Praise for *Superpowered*

"In *SUPERPOWERED*, LaVista addresses the psych. have tripped up many aspiring information technology and software development leaders. Combining the collective wisdom of 19 experts in the field with candid reflections on his own experience, he provides the reader a concise and approachable education in these "soft" skills while modeling the listening, learning, and storytelling Superpowers the book espouses. I wish I had read this 20 years ago!"
—VANCE HUNTLEY, *CTO, CONSULTANT, AND SOFTWARE EXECUTIVE*

"A great read for technology entrepreneurs and executives alike, Michael LaVista gives expert insight to business and organizational leaders on how to transform organizations as well as actively advancing a stalled career. The book is well formatted and easy to follow as the author takes you through key steps to being a better leader. *SUPERPOWERED* also helped me observe areas in my own business that could use transformation to become more tech driven and profitable."
—DR. IVAN SALABERRIOS, *DBA, CEO AND FOUNDER, AIM TECHNICAL CONSULTANTS*

"*SUPERPOWERED* has valuable and timeless leadership lessons that transcend tech and are applicable to anyone who wants to improve their leadership skills."
—SCOTT MONTY, *STRATEGIC COMMUNICATIONS AND LEADERSHIP ADVISOR*

"Using powerful stories, LaVista paints a clear picture of the successful technology leader. Grabbing these superpowers for yourself is easy and will absolutely increase your success!"
—CHARLOTTE ALLEN, *CEO AND BESTSELLING AUTHOR OF REBEL SUCCESS FOR LEADERS*

"If you are looking for the motivation, tools, and strategies to transform your company and catapult it to success, this book is definitely for you! *SUPERPOWERED* is an inspirational how-to guide that will empower you to build and inspire your tech team to reach new heights right now. LaVista interviewed experienced industry leaders and identified seven main characteristics, or superpowers, that formed the foundation for their success. In his powerful book, LaVista effectively describes those superpowers so that you, a technology leader (or emerging leader), can immediately take action to make a significant positive difference—for you, and for your organization!"
—WENDY K. BENSON, *MBA, OTR/L AND* ELIZABETH A. MYERS, *RN, CO-AUTHORS,*
THE CONFIDENT PATIENT

"Practical, insightful, inspiring and easy to follow. Directly relevant to the challenges faced in my role. Mike has included a good mix of stories and lessons from his own experience and from his clients. He sincerely provides advice that I will employ and reflect on with my team."
—GAURAV JALOTA, *CHIEF INFORMATION OFFICER, CATHOLIC EDUCATION, ARCHDIOCESE OF CANBERRA GOULBURN*

"From start to finish, *SUPERPOWERED* is filled with experiences and insights from tech industry experts. Leaders at any career stage can use these concepts to bring out the best in employees while standing out from competitors. If you're ready to level up your leadership, this book is for you!"
—MARK STEEL, *KEYNOTE SPEAKER, SALES CONSULTANT, INTERNATIONAL BESTSELLING AUTHOR*

SUPERPOWERED

MICHAEL LAVISTA

7 leadership superpowers technology executives can use to grow a more engaged, tech-driven and profitable organization

Caxy Publishing
Chicago, Illinois

Designer: Lori Malkin Ehrlich
Cover Illustration: Maurice Kessler

Michael LaVista/Caxy Publishing
212 West Van Buren Street, #1000
Chicago, IL 60607
www.caxy.com
mike@makemesuperpowered.com

Ordering Information:
Special discounts are available on quantity purchases by corporations, associations, and others. For details, contact the "Special Sales Department" at the address above.

Notice to Readers
The information in this book, along with the forms and structures provided, is meant to serve as a helpful reference guide for technology leaders.

The author of and contributors to this book take no responsibility for compliance with the laws or regulations that govern your specific business. The responsibility for making sure everything is compliant (among other things) is 100 percent yours.

Before you implement any new information or forms, please check with your own trusted business advisers, including your own attorney, to make certain that your forms and the information you plan to implement will comply with all relevant laws, customs, and regulations.

Superpowered/Michael LaVista—1st ed.
ISBN: 978-1-7355049-0-2

*To my wife, Angela, and my boys, Rocco and Blaise,
who always support me in whatever crazy
endeavor I choose to undertake.
I love you.*

■   ■   ■

Contents

So many of our dreams seem impossible, then they seem improbable, and then, when we summon the will, they soon become inevitable.

—CHRISTOPHER REEVES

Introduction

If you're like many technology executives I know, you're frustrated. Your business doesn't listen to you. Your team is hard to manage. And there's a long list of unreasonable demands piling up in your inbox.

At the same time, technology, software, and business models are all changing at light speed. To keep up, the company is asking you to complete (or in some cases initiate) its "digital transformation," i.e., to better collect, organize, and operationalize its digital assets such as data and software to advance business goals. To guide the organization to the other side, you need to be able to combine your hard technical knowledge with some specific "softer" skills that will allow you to more easily connect the dots for leadership on what needs to happen to move their agenda forward—and here's why.

This increasing dependency on technology to manage data and the activities around it means all companies that want to survive are, or are becoming, technology companies. As a technology leader, you are responsible for shepherding your firm through the transformation process, including putting in place the software required to wrangle it all.

In a perfect world, you're starting off with a desired business outcome and using that to guide what technology is required to achieve it rather than succumbing to shiny-object syndrome. This requires some discipline and exploration, which can make leadership uncomfortable—especially if they still think software development is like building a house, when it's really so much more than that.

In this new world, keeping up-to-date with technology is table stakes. To succeed longer term, you will need to be able to skillfully establish and nurture the best relationships possible with all the people you need to get the right problem-solving (and profit-making) technology in place. This book aims to show you how.

Why This Book?

This book is written specifically for CIOs, CTOs, and other technology leaders looking to take an active role in transforming their organizations, but it's also relevant to anyone who has their sights set on rising to a C-level role. And, as you will discover, one does not necessarily have to be a C-suiter to make a difference! To that end, exactly what does the founder of a software development firm, who is *not* in a CIO/CTO role, have to offer you?

My company, Caxy Interactive (www.caxy.com), gets hired by technology executives to develop, evolve, or fix mission-critical and business-critical software. We are a Chicago-based firm known for designing software that delivers specific business outcomes. Over the past 20 years, I've provided strategic software and technology advice to dozens of CIOs, CTOs, and CEOs, so I understand your role as well as the many problems and challenges you face.

I wondered if there was something I could do to help technology leaders better navigate the software development process based on our track record of success in creating outcome-based software. Then I started thinking about the technology leaders I knew who were the most successful at getting project outcomes they wanted. What was the key to their success in that role?

Conversely, I wondered what was at the root of the difficulties so many other tech leaders experienced. Why do so many technology leaders struggle to get support for their mission- and business-critical software projects and transformations?

To better understand the breadth of issues your role faces in getting software created (or fixed), I interviewed dozens of CTOs, CIOs, CEOs, COOs, and more than a few experts. The wisdom they imparted went far beyond software development. Their perspectives surprised and enlightened me, and I hope they will do the same for you.

After the interviews were done, I went back and looked for patterns, and what I found was this: in almost every case, there were seven main characteristics—I call them superpowers—that formed the foundation of their success.

The first one was mindset. In fact, mindset is the key superpower that unlocks the full potential of the six other superpowers—vision, influence, storytelling, listening, learning, and design thinking—that you need to drive change as a technology leader.

For the purpose of explanation, I've separated these superpowers into seven distinct characteristics, but the reality is there are always multiple superpowers at work simultaneously (and synergistically) when you're trying to swing a big initiative. That's why it's useful to look at each one and what it does individually, so you can focus your time and energy on shoring up whichever one is your weakest link.

Generally, the chapters are composed of three elements. Each chapter opens with a short story about how mindset or another superpower shows up in my own business. (I did that so you know I'm eating my own dog food.) Next, where applicable, I've included some thoughts from a recognized expert in the field. Most importantly, however, you'll hear from 19 of your peers who have generously shared their success strategies because they know that a rising tide lifts all boats.

In This Book

We'll begin Chapter 1 by talking about *mindset*, which is basically the super-est of all the superpowers. I've isolated it into two essential chunks, as defined by mindset expert Dr. Carol Dweck. One is the prevention vs. promotion mindset—which I know as "why we can't" vs. "how can we?"—and the other is fixed vs. growth mindset.

Growth mindset is the belief that you and the people around you can always get better at things, whereas fixed mindset is the belief that capabilities and intelligence are fixed and therefore immutable. Dweck said we all have some of each depending on the circumstances, but with conscious effort we can "grow" our growth mindset, which is key to learning new things. Our contributors have provided some great stories about mindset, as well as how to use design thinking (another superpower) to develop a growth mindset. We'll also explore another important facet of mindset at the end of the book, in Chapter 8.

In Chapter 2, we discuss the importance of the *vision super-power*—not only at the corporate level, but also at the departmental level—and why you should encourage everyone in your department to envision better ways to do things too. You'll also hear from a contributor on how knowing the business is the key to being able to see where it should go next.

Next up, in Chapter 3, is the *influence superpower*, which is the ability to affect or change someone or something in an important way by fostering trust through listening, empathy, and candor, as defined by motivational psychologist Dr. Heidi Grant. You'll also hear from several of our expert contributors on how they have acquired and used influence to build relationships and cultivate values that are key to achieving their goals.

In Chapter 4, we lay out the foundational components of the *storytelling superpower*, which is the ability to craft and tell the stories that will allow leadership to grasp how technology can advance their business objectives, so they'll be more likely to cooperate and release the resources you need to create what is necessary. This chapter contains some things you likely already know about storytelling, as well as a few new and useful things you can tuck into your tool kit. Again, you'll hear from our contributors on how they have success-fully used storytelling to get what they needed to move their outcome-focused technology projects forward.

The *listening superpower* is the topic of Chapter 5. OK, I know you know listening is important. What this chapter will hopefully do is allow you to take it to a whole new level. Listening in this context is about using all of your senses to take in and parse what is going on around you so you can communicate more effectively. It's noticing and responding to what you think others are seeing, thinking, doing, and feeling—not just what they're saying. This chapter is filled with many actionable tips about how to do just that.

Chapter 6 is all about the *learning superpower*. In this context, learning is the ability to effectively respond to an environment of constant and rapid change through the acquisition of new ideas, skills, and mindsets. To achieve this superpower, you personally have to be learning all the time, but you also have to cultivate a learning culture in your company because the ability to learn quickly and continuously is what will determine its future.

Design thinking is the final superpower and the focus of Chapter 7. According to IDEO, which first made this approach popular, design thinking is a human-centered approach to innovation that draws from the designer's tool kit to integrate the needs of people, the possibilities of technology, and the requirements for business success. Here we focus on design thinking as it applies to software development and technology, and one of our contributors will show you what that looks like in action in great detail.

In Chapter 8, we circle back to where we started, with mindset, this time through the lens of being humble in the service of leadership, which is illustrated in detail with a very special story from one of my most successful clients.

We wrap up with Chapter 9, which includes a diagnostic you can use to gauge how adept you or your organization or department is in each one of these superpowers. I also invite you to connect with me further for a deeper discussion about how we can help you use the seven superpowers to improve your software development outcomes.

Writing this book has been a journey, and I have done everything possible to ensure it is a worthwhile investment of your time. I hope I've succeeded and that you enjoy the ride. Comments? Feedback? I'd love to hear your thoughts. Email me at mike@makemesuperpowered.com.

OK. Ready to start naming and claiming your seven superpowers? Great. Let's get started.

VISION

DESIGN THINKING

INFLUENCE

MINDSET

LEARNING

STORYTELLING

LISTENING

Mindset

When I first started Caxy Interactive, all the work the company did was $5,000. Want a website? $5,000. Want a lead-generation system? $5,000. Want a kiosk app? $5,000. Why $5,000? It was the most money I could imagine anyone spending on something ever. Never mind that what it cost me to do the job was at least that much—and usually more. I swore that all anyone would ever pay us was $5,000. I was stuck in "why we can't" mode and it was slowly suffocating my business.

One day, I was asked to bid on a very complex project. One that could really do something for the business. Out of desperation, I created a proposal for $18,000. I was convinced the prospect would never go for it, but this project was way bigger than our average job, and it was just going to take more. I dreaded the negotiation and wondered how we'd ever be able to do it for $5,000 in the end—and still stay in business.

Did the client reject the proposal? Push back and demand a discount? Nope. They signed it without hesitation. I was elated (once I recovered from the shock)—and then I got curious. What if my belief that $5,000 was the most anyone would ever pay for something was *wrong*? Would other clients pay $18,000, or even more? What if we and the client aligned ourselves around the value of what the work was supposed to deliver to the company? The next job I quoted was

$20,000. Then, for a while, everything was a $20,000 job. And then I decided to start charging however much it would cost to deliver the outcome the client wanted, no matter if that amount was $50,000, $100,000, or $1,000,000. The work kept coming, and the projects got bigger and more complex. Charging more allowed me to hire top talent and move projects forward faster, so the ability to deliver value at those levels increased with our fees.

If I hadn't been forced to manually override my "why we can't" mindset and send out that proposal for $18,000, Caxy would likely still be doing $5,000 websites—if we still existed.

Over time, I realized there was a one-to-one relationship between what I believed and what I achieved. In the words of social activist Mahatma Gandhi, "Your beliefs become your thoughts, your thoughts become your words, your words become your actions, your actions become your habits, your habits become your values, your values become your destiny." The point is it all starts with what you believe, because your beliefs determine your mindset.

That said, there are a lot of ways mindset plays out. You may have a "how can we?" mindset in one area and a "why we can't" mindset in another. The goal here is to make you aware of it so ultimately you can make a proactive choice rather than being forced from one side to the other like I was.

> ↗ The *mindset superpower* is the ability to oper-
> ate from the mindset that serves you best,
> including the ability to solve problems by asking "how
> can we?" rather than focusing on "why we can't."

Prevention vs. Promotion Mindsets

The objection "why we can't" is an example of a *prevention* mindset, while the approach "how can we?" is an example of a *promotion* mind-set. Dr. Heidi Grant and Dr. E. Tory Higgins talk about the differences between these two mindsets in their book, *Focus: Use Different Ways of Seeing the World for Success and Influence.*

People with a promotion mindset see their goals as opportunities for *gain* or *advancement.* In other words, they are focused on all the great things that will happen when they succeed—the benefits and rewards. They play to win. People with a prevention mindset tend to see their goals as opportunities to *meet* their responsibilities and stay safe. They consider what might go wrong if they don't work hard enough to achieve something. They don't play to win—they play to *not lose.*[1]

The question "how can we?" is so powerful because it is at the foundation of all creativity and innovation. The belief that change is possible—that we have or can obtain the means by which to make something better—underpins all problem-solving.

Eventually, I started to realize that all my clients fell into one of these two mindsets (at least when it came to software development). Either they were afraid to make any moves for fear of failure ("why we can't") or they were constantly challenging their beliefs in service of growth ("how can we?").

So many people operate from the "why we can't" mindset yet also expect their businesses to grow. I'm not sure how that's possible, especially if all you're doing is making a case that what you need to be doing to grow can't be done. (Meanwhile, trust me, your competitor is out there doing all of it—and more.) Not sure if you have a prevention mindset? Here are a few tells:

- "We just don't have the budget."
- "That's a next-year question."
- "We just don't have the people."
- "And how would we do that?"

All of those are code for "I'm not willing to risk looking foolish in front of leadership or drawing unnecessary attention to myself."

- "We can't beat competitor X."
- "Our industry is declining."
- "Our customers will never do X."
- "That will never work."

These statements are code for "I'm not willing to risk trying to increase our influence over our effect on competitors, our industry standing, or our relationships with customers because what if I'm wrong?"

If you are stuck in "why we can't" mode, the good news is you can nudge yourself (and others) toward a promotion mindset. The first step is to model that "how can we?" mindset to others.

There's a contagious energy to the "how can we?" mindset because it's about the dream. It's about what you, your department, or your company could be as opposed to what you are now. It gets you, your team, and hopefully leadership thinking about the future and the outcomes needed to create it. It's inspiring. Talking about what could be evokes the spirit of other big goals. Take, for example, President John F. Kennedy's belief that there was a way to get boots on the moon by the end of the 1960s, or Jeff Bezos's belief that he could transform Amazon from a money-loser to the world's most technologically advanced online marketplace.

The key to success is to focus your energy and attention on "how can we?" For example, when Olympic downhill skiers are heading down a mountain, they don't look for the trees. They know if they do they'll run into one at 100 miles per hour. Instead, they look for the snow. All the successful technology executives I spoke with also look for the "snow." It's not that they don't know the trees are there; they just focus on navigating around them.

In the following story, my client and friend Sarah Isaacs, founder and COO of Chicago-based Conventus Corporation was faced with a puzzling lack of traction for a new security-vendor point solution that everyone said they loved. It would have been easy for her to blame the failure on the customer's lack of vision, but instead she applied a "how can we?" approach to solving the problem. This approach led her to adjust the use case to match her customer's real priorities and values and "swizzle" the product offering into what is now known as North-Star Navigator, an enterprise risk-based vulnerability-management tool. Here is her story.

Use Case Swizzle

Sarah Isaacs

After years of working as consultants implementing, configuring, and training on large security-vendor point solutions, we realized everyone was having the same problem in that almost no one could tell us which machines or systems needed these security solutions installed.

Clients said things like, "Jim left a couple years ago and didn't update the database," or "Oh, I have a spreadsheet that's outdated, but nobody really looks at it." We thought we'd discovered a golden opportunity and so we designed some new tools to help clients gather the information needed to have a comprehensive asset inventory.

Everybody we talked to in security said, "Oh, this is awesome. This is what I need. I can't believe you do this. It's so comprehensive."

The problem was we could not find a buyer for it. Why? Because there was no line item for it in any budget! Security needed it to do their job, but they wanted someone else to buy it, manage it, and feed that information across the company.

There are a lot of reasons companies succeed and fail, but if you don't have a buyer for your product—even if it is spectacular, and this was—it's a dead end.

So we went back to the drawing board to figure out how we could either change the product or change our story about the product to match something that does have a line item. The answer: vulnerability management.

The basis of a vulnerability-management product is that you have to be able to see what you're protecting—your assets—before you can prioritize what to fix first.

And vulnerability management is something that every enterprise organization budgets for, whether it is a service they pay for externally, a product they purchase and manage in-house, or a whole team dedicated to monitoring it.

So we "swizzled" our use case and tweaked our product to fit those needs, and then we went to market that way instead. And we were right on time with this pivot—the number of vulnerabilities has more than doubled in the past five years and that has been a wake-up call for a lot of organizations. ▲

■　■　■

Here's another example of how a promotion mindset in our culture sets us apart. A few years ago we got pulled into a contest framed as a "hackathon" by a major corporation. This company had some new technology it wasn't sure what to do with, and 10 developers took it up on the challenge to build some novel apps and explore how the new technology could be used. The company said, "OK, here are a couple of pages of documentation and an API. Come back in two weeks and show us what you've got."

We put a team together based on who was available and interested, brainstormed about seven or eight ideas, and then narrowed it to five apps. At the last minute, we added a sixth.

We later found out that out of 10 teams, just seven apps were turned in and six of them were ours. Only one other team got the API working. Eight others complained about how it didn't work. The point of this story is that our approach to the project was, "This sounds fun. Let's make it work. Let's make something!" It was that promotion mindset that opened everyone's mind. (There were also prizes.) We continued to work with the company on this API for a couple of years afterward, which made a good relationship even stronger.

It might sound like a promotion mindset is the only one you should use when it comes to business success, but nothing could be further from the truth. The next story is from John Scholvin, former CTO of a Chicago-based proprietary stock-trading firm and a field consultant at a Boston-based enterprise data software vendor. It's a great example of constructive use of the prevention mindset and when to override it.

Pragmatic Pessimism
John Scholvin

My baseline tendency is pessimism. And that has served me well because, frankly, a lot of my career has been about identifying worst-case scenarios and paying attention to risk. I'm looking at the tail. I am looking at the three- and four-sigma events out there sometimes.

But you have to be supercareful to not be that pessimistic guy in the idea-generation phase. Nothing sucks more than the guy in the room whose response to everything is, "We can't do that. It's hard." That said, there does come a point when some pretty black-and-white implementation decisions are required, a time to say, "OK, this isn't going to work; this thing you want to do is not something we can feasibly do." But you can't do that too early. You want to start out projects being an optimist, and then, as you get deeper into the implementation details, become more and more pessimistic.

That's part of working in trading. You can literally *never* stop thinking about risk—trading risk, platform risk, security risk, even risk of failure to deliver something. If that's not keeping you up at night, you will blow up at some point. It's got to be there, but you can't let it dominate your thinking. 👤

■ ■ ■

There is a rule in improvisational comedy that you have to accept what the other actors are doing and use it in a "yes, and" fashion. That means you use what they have put into the scene, but you work with it and extend it. In business we apply that rule to the brainstorming part of the process. In the beginning, all ideas are good and welcome. In either scenario, a "no" or "that won't work" in the beginning stages will snuff out the fire.

Scholvin's story shows that starting out with an inclusive mindset is the way to get ideas going. Later, you can apply pragmatic pessimism to focus on the ideas and come up with what to actually work on.

Fixed vs. Growth Mindsets

Another lens you can look through to understand mindset is fixed vs. growth, as defined by American psychologist Dr. Carol Dweck in her 2007 book, *Mindset: The New Psychology of Success*. Dr. Heidi Grant, a student of Dweck's, defines it as "be good" vs. "get better." You can also think of it as dynamic vs. static, or innate ability vs. consistent effort.

According to Dweck, we all have some of each mindset in different areas. The growth mindset—the belief that you can *get better*—opens the door to the ability to address the complications and obstacles inherent in managing and developing technology with a "how can we?" attitude. Fixed mindset language sounds like this:

- "Person X will never learn Y."
- "You can't teach an old dog new tricks."
- "I'm not a good storyteller/learner/listener."
- "I'm no visionary."
- "I can't influence anyone."
- "That's not how we do it here."
- "I'm too old/young to do X."

Any time you find yourself attaching a limiting label to something or someone—including yourself—chances are you're operating from a fixed mindset. To someone with a fixed mindset, who you are, what your company is and does, is perceived as immutable. They believe the abilities and characteristics of people and things are fixed and thus unable to get better. "It is what it is" is the mantra of the fixed mindset. Conversely, a growth mindset sounds like this:

- "How could person X learn Y?"
- "How could I become a good storyteller/learner/listener?"
- "How can I be more visionary?"
- "How can I increase my influence on leadership?"

A person operating from a growth mindset perceives themselves and others as being capable of growing and changing—as able to get better—and, as a result, feels some agency in their ability to do something to help make that happen.

Operating from a growth mindset doesn't mean everything always works the way you think it should. Getting better often involves adjusting your strategy and trying a number of different approaches until you find something that works.

That said, the concept of fixed vs. growth mindset is trendy, so you'll want to keep a lookout for false growth mindset. Dweck called out these "misunderstandings" in her book. "Many people take what they like about themselves and call it a 'growth mindset,'" she said. According to Dweck, there's a difference between being flexible or open-minded and being dedicated to growing one's talent. The other misunderstanding is that many people believe a growth mindset is only about effort or praising effort when it is also about trying new strategies and seeking help and input from others when needed.

Shifting from Fixed to Growth Mindset

Remember, according to Dweck, we all have a little of both types of mindset—fixed and growth. The good news is that we can shift. No, a fixed mindset cannot be surgically removed and replaced with a growth mindset. The key is to develop the new belief alongside the old one.

As the growth mindset gets stronger over time, it will provide you with more choices about how to think, feel, and act. Doing this confronts the basic assumption many "hard chargers" make, which is that traits (e.g., intelligence, motivation, or capabilities)—theirs and others—are fixed. This traps them in a framework of judgment rather than one of growth. The goal is to change "the internal monologue from a judging one to a growth-oriented one," said Dweck.

Perhaps the biggest shift from fixed to growth mindset for me was the day after I bought out my business partner, Clint Cox. In the first few years of Caxy Interactive, I led development and my partner ran sales and accounts. Those were the skills that we had at the time, but we thought of them more as who we were. I was a programming type of person, and he was a sales-and-accounts type of person. He got a thrill out of calling new customers, which I was amazed by.

But then, all of a sudden, we didn't have a sales or account person anymore. My first "solution" was to briefly consider if we really even needed those kinds of people and roles. (I quickly realized that we did!)

My first impulse was to hire for those roles, but then I got curious and wondered, "Hmmm. Is this something I could do? Something I could learn to do even if I have no experience?" I invested a huge amount of time in reading, coaching, and trial and error. And, little by little, I got better. And, little by little, I even liked it. Maybe a lot.

I see that transition—from the fixed mindset of "I'm a programming guy" to the growth mindset of "I can learn to do sales and manage accounts"—as foundational to the business evolving into what it is today, a company that's not only about building technology, but also about understanding how to identify outcomes and create the technology that will allow clients to achieve them.

A Growth Mindset Is Antifragile

A growth mindset also allows you to capitalize on the antifragile characteristics found in Nassim Taleb's book, *Antifragile: Things That Gain from Disorder*. The author wondered why unpredictable events caused some organizations to crash, while others seemed to get stronger. *Antifragile* breaks down different systems into three categories:

- **Fragile:** systems that get weaker when unexpected events happen. For example, a wineglass is fragile. It will break if you drop it. But it will also break if you put it in the dishwasher sideways, or if you just nick it in the wrong way. The point is once it's broken, it stays broken.
- **Robust:** systems that don't change when something unexpected happens. An example is dropping a bowling ball onto a pillow; the bowling ball doesn't get any stronger or weaker from the fall.
- **Antifragile:** systems that get stronger under stress and strain. An example is lifting weights, which breaks down muscle tissue in the moment, but builds it up even stronger.[2]

An antifragile idea is one that only gets stronger and grows the more you beat it up. The growth mindset aspect of this idea is in the belief that if we're willing to put up with some stress (i.e., concerted effort, creativity, and asking for or accepting help), we can get better at getting better.

Businesses aren't made of glass, but many leaders treat them that way. There are a lot of brittle beliefs that make it impossible for the organization to get better—impossible for it to change. The problem is businesses that can't change eventually die. To make your business (or department or processes) more antifragile, look for ways to test the edges by purposely stressing certain areas in a strategic (and manageable) way. Beyond fragility, businesses and ideas tend to rot if left unexamined and unchanged.

One example from the *Antifragile* book is what Taleb called the Barbell Strategy. This strategy calls for an organization to put 85 to 90 percent of its resources into core business activities and the rest into high-risk, high-reward activities. From a technology perspective, that might mean assigning 85 to 90 percent of resources to core apps and services, and 15 to 20 percent to research and development—Skunk Works projects.

You don't have to go crazy. If you were strength training in the gym, your first test might be the leg press set 25 pounds heavier than what you're used to—not attempting to move a 10-ton rock.

Developing a Growth Mindset through Design Thinking

Another effective way to shift from fixed to growth mindset (and to help others do so as well) is by embracing design thinking. Design-thinking ideas began to emerge in the 1960s, but design-firm IDEO was the first to show its design process in the 1990s. IDEO defines design thinking as "a human-centered approach to innovation—anchored in understanding a customer's needs, rapid prototyping, and generating creative ideas—that will transform the way you develop products, services, processes, and organizations."[3]

To be successful in design thinking demands a growth mindset. Jeanne Liedtka, Randy Salzman, and Daisy Azer, coauthors of the 2017 book *Design Thinking for the Greater Good: Innovation in the Social Sector*, said in a blog post, "Design thinking is a tool for innovation in the corporate world and, increasingly, the social sector. In fact, what makes design thinking good for problem-solving is also good for personal and professional growth. This is because design thinking embodies what Carol Dweck referred to as the growth mindset. With curiosity, effort, and practice, we can design better outcomes for ourselves and others."[4]

■ ■ ■

At Caxy, when working with clients to produce something new, we love to pull back from the proposed product and execution that clients typically show up with and find the customer pain or desire that supports it. If you want to hit a home run with a digital product and you're not thinking about the customer first, you're going to strike out.

In our business, we constantly look at what our clients' pain points are and how we're currently solving them. We evaluate our product and service mix to see if there are areas that clients soak up as quickly as we can produce them and others that seem to land with a thud. We experiment and try new things, always in service of trying to understand how we can serve our clients better. (We'll talk about design thinking in more detail in Chapter 7.)

In this next story, Rachel Higham, former managing director of IT for a major telecommunications company and current CIO of WPP, describes how using a design-thinking approach known as "grizzlies" helped a team of software engineers not only shift from fixed to growth mindset, but also become ambassadors for the design-thinking process.

Overcoming Resistance with Grizzlies

Rachel Higham

During our IT transformation program at the telecommunications company, we developed a technique called "grizzlies," named after the bear. It's anything that will slow you down, growl at you, take your ankles out, or eat you alive as you go forward on your transformation journey.

The technique is quite simple: you brainstorm and name possible grizzlies before you meet them on the trail and then solve for them ahead of time. Naming them removes the surprise and the initial emotional reaction when you do encounter them. By thinking ahead about what you might do should you encounter one, you already have a game plan.

A significant grizzly we encountered during our design-thinking boot-camp training program was resistance to change. Would a team of software engineers that had a structured, analytical mindset really get on board with creative techniques that required them to draw cartoons or use Legos? After identifying the grizzly in our training planning sessions, we decided to film the experience of our first set of boot campers, and put in that first boot camp every single grumpy detractor we could find. We then used the video diaries to create a high-energy montage that we played relentlessly throughout our organization. You know you are winning when you have somebody who was vocally being skeptical about the approach appear on camera and say, "I didn't know what to expect, but this has completely changed the way I think about my customer and my outcomes."

It just snowballed from there. We kept telling those stories of the mindsets we shifted, and the excitement and acceptance of our new ways of working just kept on building. Then, as we started applying design thinking to solving problems in our daily work, we created *Our Stories*—beautiful, graphical case studies that told the story of how our technique was applied and how the outcome was massively uplifted. We shared wonderful quotations from customers, our team, and the design-thinking coaches that described the personal journey they had been on, and they became one of the most powerful features of the stories.

Over three years we built a digital library of more than 30 stories, and it was a great source of pride for our team to be featured in one. Many of our original skeptics flipped to become change ambassadors and even design-thinking coaches—and their Lego skills are fantastic too! They go and speak to their colleagues and customers about the difference design thinking is making and have even inspired many of our partner organizations to adopt the practice too. 👤

■ ■ ■

This can-do, find-a-way mentality is what unlocks the full potential of the seven superpowers—mindset, vision, influence, storytelling, listening, learning, and design thinking—that you need to move mountains.

It's my belief that you can grow and change. And don't worry, you don't have to be a 10 at all seven superpowers right away. You just have to consistently work your way forward. My contributors and I, through this book, aim to show you how.

Summary: Mindset

■ The *mindset superpower* is the ability to operate from the mindset that serves you best, including the ability to solve problems by asking "how can we?" rather than explaining "why we can't."

■ People with a promotion mindset see their goals as opportunities for gain or advancement. In other words, they are focused on all the great things that will happen for them when they succeed—the benefits and rewards. They play to win.

■ People with a prevention mindset tend to see their goals as opportunities to meet their responsibilities and stay safe. They play not to lose.

■ A growth mindset is the belief that you can get better with concentrated effort and help.

■ A fixed mindset is the belief that abilities and characteristics of people and things are fixed and thus unable to get better.

■ To shift from a fixed mindset to a growth mindset, you have to confront the belief that certain traits are fixed and work to shift the internal monologue from a judging one to a growth-oriented one.

■ We all have some of each mindset; it's a matter of being aware and making the mental shift.

■ An antifragile idea is one that only gets stronger and grows the more you beat it up. The growth mindset aspect of this idea is the belief that if you're willing to put up with some stress (i.e., concerted effort, creativity, and asking for and accepting help), you can get stronger at getting better.

■ An effective way to shift from fixed to growth mindset (and to help others do so as well) is by embracing design thinking.

Vision

One chilly Saturday morning, I was holding my baby boy, staring out the window of our South Loop condo, and contemplating some fun plans my wife had made for us, when my cell phone rang. On the other end of the line was a major client, calling to alert me to a serious production issue.

I thought for a minute about who I could hand this problem off to, but I knew there was no one. I didn't trust anyone enough to follow through. I had to tell my wife I'd need to beg off the family fun (and not for the first time). I spent the rest of the weekend working on the problem myself.

I knew a lot of small-business entrepreneurs, and they worked all the time too. Our significant others all hated it, but our refrain was always, "What else do you want me to do?" What they wanted us to do, of course, was figure out a way to change and make it better.

And so, in January 2005, I set a goal to do just that. I decided to believe things could be different, that the company could change, and so could I. With that belief, I shifted from a fixed mindset about my business—i.e., "This is just the way it is when you own your own company"—to a growth mindset—"With focused effort, and some resources and support, my company and I could change. We could *get better*." I started to envision what the company could become, how we could differentiate, and how we could provide long-lasting value for our clients.

For the longest time we were focused solely on doing great work. We were software *artisans*. Our strategy was to earn trust with clients by doing an exceptional job. Our thinking was that doing great work would create goodwill in the market and our platinum reputation would attract new clients. We were Chicago's best-kept software development secret—and we were stuck.

By waiting for clients to discover us, we were reacting to the market. And even when they did find us, we continued our habit of reacting, this time to the work they brought. This habit often meant we developed solutions the clients thought they wanted, but weren't necessarily the best thing for their businesses to focus on at that time. We were also starting to feel the pinch of competition, not only domestically, but also from developers overseas.

To stand out, I knew we needed to become known as a firm that could help technology and business leaders sort through the landscape of ideas and objectives. We needed to be trusted advisers who could provide expert guidance on the best ways to employ technology to reach objectives—before the first line of code was written.

To achieve this goal, we needed better people—people who were not only better programmers, but also wanted to both learn and teach. We needed a group of people who wanted to work as a team rather than a collection of individuals clicking away all day in isolation.

More importantly, if I was going to grow this company, I needed there to be someone other than me who a client could call for technical support in the event of a Saturday morning emergency.

Within about six months, there were a lot of new faces at the company, and a number of people had self-selected out of the new vision. (As it turns out, the commitment to quality and collaboration is not for everyone.) Around the same time, I began to overcome my fear of sales, and I started having meaningful (and more proactive) conversations that quickly led to better and more profitable work.

■ ■ ■

Ask 12 business leaders what their definition of *vision* is and you'll get 12 different answers. Most of the time people talk about vision in terms of a *vision statement*. Let's set levels. Let's agree that to have a vision is to have conceived of a desired future state of business. According to Kirstin O'Donovan, a certified life and productivity coach and founder and CEO of Top Results Coaching, a vision statement is the articulation of that vision so it can be communicated to others inside the business.

For example, Tesla's vision statement is "to create the most compelling car company of the 21st century by driving the world's transition to electric vehicles."[1] Before Tesla could write that statement, however, Elon Musk first needed to conceive of what he wanted Tesla to become.

A technology leader's vision is the conception of a desired, improved future state that technology helps create. An example would be to provide the most secure platform for customers to manage their financial lives through modern, scalable technology. The problem is that leadership's vision doesn't always take technology into consideration.

> **The *vision superpower* is the ability to conceive of a situation or state in which technology could move an organization significantly closer to its overall desired state.**

The vision superpower is about knowing the business well enough that you can imagine what is possible with technology. Your challenge then is to influence leadership to start thinking of technology in terms of its potential to create significant positive financial outcomes for the business and stop thinking of it only in terms of budget and cost. It's one thing to conceive of the future state. To get the buy-in is another story, and you'll need to leverage your other superpowers to do it.

Leadership (hopefully) has a clear vision for what the organization wants to become and has created a compelling mission statement and a strategy they believe can effectively advance that agenda.

Why Is Your Vision for Technology So Important?

So many CIO/CTO roles are stuck in mere mortal mode, despite the fact that the business would benefit so much more from a super-powered approach. Perhaps you are operating with a static budget and expectations that your main job is to keep email working and servers up. Or maybe you're given a budget for investments in people, products, and systems, and then leadership starts pressuring you to spend less on those items because they perceive them as overhead or OPEX.

So you find a cheaper way to do email, figure out how to do more with fewer people, and get some cost savings in the cloud. The financial outcome you can deliver here is efficiency, and that's worth something. The problem is it's a zero-sum game. At some point, you'll have put in the most cost-effective systems, cut the people you can cut, and move all the things you can into the cloud. The next time leadership comes to you for cuts, there will be no blood left in the stone. Then what?

To add to this problem, if your organization is like most others, everyone from your C-suite and internal teams to your customers and users expect your technology to not only always work, but also be at least as good as any other technology they encounter in or outside the office.

You know this as the Amazon Effect. Because of Amazon, we expect to be able to purchase and receive just about any item we desire within a day or two. What most people forget is Amazon lost tons of money at first, and for a long time it wasn't clear whether it would ever be profitable. Even today, Amazon reinvests practically all its profits back into the company.[2]

Jeff Bezos's vision for Amazon is "to be Earth's most customer-centric company, where customers can find and discover anything they might want to buy online."[3] A mountain of investors' money over a couple of decades has led to an ever-improving set of systems that has made Amazon the mind-bogglingly efficient behemoth it is today.

Few companies have Amazon-level resources, and they probably can't afford to operate at a loss for decades either. Still, when it comes to technology user experience and performance, you're held to the same standards. You're expected to get results and work miracles fast with limited resources, while playing whack-a-mole with existing customer issues, infrastructure problems, security, and so on. It's an endlessly spinning hamster wheel.

The good news is there's a way to start down a more strategic path. The first step is to claim the vision superpower. The vision superpower is about conceiving of ways to manage technology investments to achieve financial outcomes. You'll want to amplify the vision superpower by activating the "how can we?" mindset we talked about in Chapter 1.

This mindset is about envisioning a future technology state that will move the company toward its vision as efficiently and effectively as possible. As a technology leader, you must be able to identify those opportunities that nontechnical people can't see, and then you need to be able to communicate the potential of those opportunities in a way they can understand and support. To do so, said Rusty Kennington, CIO for building-solutions provider Henry Company, you need to know the business.

Know the Business

Rusty Kennington

I want everyone on my team to not only know what the company does and how it makes money, but also have some experience in how the company operates. That is the best place to learn the language of the business.

For example, one of my roles was with Brinker, a restaurant company that owned several different brands, including Maggiano's, Chili's, and On the Border. I worked in the kitchen for a day and in the front of the house for a day in every single brand—and everyone on my team did too. When I worked for a steel company, I worked in the steel mill for a week. In my role at Corsicana Mattress Company, I visited customers. The more you engage and learn how things work, the more natively you speak the language of that business.

Being intuitive about what you do as a company adds to the tool kit that you have—in other words, the technology capabilities—and that's what gives you that unique voice in the boardroom, C-suite, or any conversation about the art of the possible. If you're not in that conversation, a lot of those ideas don't make it to the table.

I first learned the importance of understanding the business right out of college, when I spent the first year after school working in construction to pay for it. I was a laborer, a low guy on the totem pole. It was a big job, a building on 42nd Street and Park Avenue in New York City. All of the electricians, and most of the tradesmen, knew I was a college kid. A lot of them took me under their wing. One day, one of the master electricians came to me and said, "Hey, kid, come here." He pointed to the ceiling and said, "When you get to designing a new house as an electrical engineering major, don't design that." He pointed up to the ceiling, which was still concrete, and said, "Why do you think I'm telling you that?" I could see that the conduit was really jammed into these hard angles right in the corner, and it was near a bunch of other pipes. I said, "Well, how do you get to it?" He said, "Exactly."

And so I learned early on to think about what we do on paper and how it's going to end up in the field.

Another example is my first real job, which was for General Dynamics. I was supporting engineering and manufacturing. My office was in a building five miles away from where the F-16s were made. I got a chance to go get a desk in the plant, and I jumped on it. I became much more intuitive about what solutions were needed because I was involved in so many more drive-by conversations with people in the plant. The plant supervisor would pick me up and take me for a ride down the floor and say, "Look at this."

I learned that I enjoyed speaking both languages. I saw it as an imperative. How can you really be effective as a technology leader if you can't speak the language of the actual business and you don't really know how things work?

So, when I got to Corsicana, I already knew the first step to success was doing whatever was required to understand and become an expert in what we did as a business. That meant understanding how we made money and, in our case, as a manufacturer of mattresses, how our customers made money, as well as all the aspects of how we served those customers.

IT is one of the few departments in the company that sees everything and sees it very intimately because our systems support it all. Our job is really to make sure the technology engine is running well. If it's not, we've got no voice, and there's no reason for management to listen to any of our new ideas.

From an employee standpoint, I'm also responsible for making sure everyone knows what we do as a company. I'm not telling them how to write in Python or how to configure the firewall; they're going to be smarter than me in those areas anyway. But I'm telling them first what we do as a business and where the challenges are, and then what we're doing about it.

For example, everything we did at Corsicana was from the customer inward. We completely rebuilt what the customer-service internals looked like to change the customer experience. So, instead of enabling an agent to answer every call and process that customer's information, we started to look at what most customers were actually calling about. It turned out that roughly 70 percent of the calls were customers wanting to know when their mattress would be delivered.

As a consumer, we have a tracking number. We know when FedEx is coming. But when it came to an 18-wheeler full of mattresses stopping at five or six different stores across 400 miles, nobody knew how to track that. And so we started doing it. We knew by the phone number who the customer was. The system we created automatically checked to see if that customer had a delivery en route. If they did, the system told them the current estimated delivery time and then said, "Press one if you still want to speak to an agent." The result was less work for our customer service representatives and much, much happier customers. ♟

■　■　■

Picture this: your company capturing or creating a more than $100 million-a-year market based on your new technology. Can you make the case that your company should spend $10 million to get there? Would that be a good investment? What are the chances it would work or not? If you listened to customers and continued to improve that technology, both of those numbers—what the company is willing to invest and what outcomes it will experience—would likely grow.

The technology you create would need to differentiate the business with new, unique, and ownable services or experiences. If you create something that competitors can't offer (at least not now), the value of that innovation is as big as the market it can capture.

Knowing your firm's desired financial outcomes will allow you to approach things differently than if you are simply given a static budget to operate. In fact, problem-solving to get to a specific financial outcome should provide you with the leverage you need to get the funds required to move forward. It then becomes about your ability to influence stakeholders and the stories you tell. (More information on how that works will appear in Chapters 3 and 4.)

Here's the thing: most companies don't start with a financial outcome they want to achieve; they start with a problem they want to fix or something they want to build. It could be an app or a new customer portal, or maybe they want to create a better way to report on their data. They then have tons of questions about what features should be included, but there's one question that rarely gets asked: Is it actually worth it to do this project? How do I know this? In 20 years of building software solutions, I can think of only a handful of clients who showed up asking this question first.

This question might not be overtly stated, but you are likely getting the answer indirectly. For example, a business says "no thanks" to a project you proposed after you tell them how much it's going to cost. What happened? The person you pitched the project to made a mental calculation that it was not going to be worth it. But based on what? In the meantime, to get to that number, you did a lot of legwork with vendors and partners, talked to your team, made your own calculations, and burned a lot of organizational time and energy.

That's why you always need to start the conversation with this question: "What financial outcome is this project supposed to achieve?"

Let's say the answer is to grow a certain customer segment. Don't stop there. Ask, "How much is it supposed to grow? By when? What other things have to happen to make that real?"

In my experience, if the expected financial outcome is 10 times the investment to do it, you can get management on board. Even better, what if you calculated what it would cost to *not* have that outcome?

Psychologists Daniel Kahneman and Amos Tversky coined the term *loss aversion* to describe how people choose to avoid a loss over taking a gain. Once the business stakes are made clear, you'll get whiplash from how quickly things get approved.

If the outcome is about the same or less than the investment, it will be a tougher sell. There are probably better investments to make.

In my experience, most companies have a long backlog of projects that they theoretically have committed to doing. But that list seems to languish and many of the projects have been sitting there for months, or even years. Why? Typically, the backlog is full of obvious projects that everyone else seems to be doing, so now your company wants to do them too. They ended up on a list without deliberate consideration, and now they are in limbo because the business case to do them is not there. Management can feel it subconsciously, but they haven't acted on removing the projects or going forward with them because a clear case hasn't been made or even attempted. If you have such a list, take a look at it now and clear your mental load by making the case for *not* doing some of those old projects.

Let me give you an example. A client I was working with recently wanted to build a portal for customers to be able to pay their bills more easily. As we talked through the idea and what it would take, it became clear that while the current system for paying a bill was a little clunky and required some manual effort on the part of the receivables team, it worked well enough. The best outcome we could come up with for doing the project was freeing up some of the receivables clerk's time. And it wasn't going to be cheap to do it.

As we kept talking and searching for worthy outcomes, we uncovered another problem that sounded like it was worth fixing. Long ago, when the business was smaller, it got into the habit of fronting payments on behalf of customers for third-party servicers. The customers appreciated the low-friction service calls and would pay the company back and it was all very manageable. The company took a small percentage for facilitating these payments, so it was even a profit center—in theory. But as the business grew, the amount it was fronting on behalf of customers grew as well, which created new problems—and new worries. What if there was a problem with the service? What if the customer had a dispute or didn't pay the company back?

The financial outcome this client wanted to achieve was to have a predictable profit margin based on a known volume of service calls while cutting costs to achieve it. We came up with the idea of a payment portal where servicers could post invoices and customers could make payments in a way that didn't require any manual intervention or floating payments. It would pay for itself in a matter of months and create a low-effort income stream more or less in perpetuity.

According to a 2019 study by global consulting firm Korn Ferry, the average tenure of a CIO is just 4.6 years.[4] It takes an average of five years for a company to complete its digital transformation.[5] So, if you don't make it a priority to become known by your C-level colleagues as a strategic partner who can bring some vision to the table right now, you may not be around to reap the benefits of your hard work.

To prevent this outcome from happening, you need to take a few steps. The first one, as my friend Rusty Kennington articulated, is to familiarize yourself with the business. How does it make money? How does the current technology stack help or hinder that process? To that end, what are the opportunities and threats in your marketplace?

Once you understand the industry landscape, then you need to find out what leadership is trying to do. What does your CEO measure? What do your CFO, COO, and other executives and stakeholders measure? How can you partner with the CEO and CFO to create a plan that specifies a financial outcome for technology investments that aligns with business goals?

For example, if a business has a goal of trying to attract 20 percent more customers in the next 12 months with a revenue goal of $X million and a margin goal of Y percent, what technology solution could you envision that would accelerate or even transform that process?

Finally, you also need to understand what your customers and users want from your technology. (Remember the Amazon Effect?) You may need to increase your exposure to them so you can hear and interpret what they say firsthand. (More information about that will appear in Chapter 5, where we will talk about the listening superpower.)

By working with the business to understand where it is truly going, and actively contributing to what it could become, you'll reposition yourself as someone whose vision and insights are strategically valuable and, eventually, critical to the business.

You also may want to engage your staff to see what they have to say in terms of technology potential. Following is a story from consultant David Srour, about a middle manager he encountered on a project who had a vision of his own.

Vision Is Where You Find It
David Srour

You actually don't have to be a CIO or CTO to have a vision and make a difference. I'll give you an example. There was a guy in Chicago who worked for a big real estate company and drove the back-office transformation for some public REITs. He wasn't a senior executive; he was in the middle of the mix. What he did have, however, was a vision.

At the time (2005), the company was reporting on a cash basis and was running a custom accounting program written in Basic and running on a DEC VAX system. He knew technology was advancing and began asking questions. "What's our competition doing? Why? Why is that important to us, even though we've been in the same place for 30 years and are very successful in that place?" He also networked externally and found out what other people were doing. He then brought in people to tell those stories, first to his colleagues and then to upper management. He initiated a process and quantified its value to the point that it was transferred to the CIO for implementation.

Since then, the company has advanced substantially. But it was kicked forward by one guy who had a vision based on what he saw in the market and began gathering interest around it.

Vision, wherever it originates, is important, but ultimately it's the team executing that vision that drives the success. Whether that success is easier or harder will be determined by that team. The right team—meaning one with a diversity of approaches, ideas, and backgrounds—will result in easier success in most cases. ▲

■ ■ ■

Another obstacle you might run into is that your vision for what technology can do for the firm is ahead of what senior management is able to envision. In that case, you have some work to do. Here are some wise words from Ilyce Glink, CEO of Best Money Moves: "You have to be in position with your idea and your thought leadership, and then the world has to catch up with you. You need to focus on changing hearts and minds by connecting the dots. Tell your story over and over again with such conviction that people finally start to listen and see what is there for them. This is the hard work of educating your audience ahead of a trend. You will spend a lot of time and money doing it, but if you're successful, you will define the market."

■ ■ ■

Summary: Vision

■ The *vision superpower* is your ability to conceive of a situation or state in which technology could move the organization significantly closer to its overall desired state.

■ Vision is about changing from one state to another; to achieve it, one must believe that change is possible. Mindset is that belief. Mindset unlocks the ability to envision an ambitious future.

■ Vision is where you find it. Ask around!

Influence

I was now one guy with a clear proactive vision, with a company full of people and clients acquired during the previous reactive period.

To make my vision real, I needed team members who also believed in that vision and were willing to adapt what they were doing so everyone was pulling in the same (right) direction. I also needed to figure out how to get clients (new and old) to trust my new approach, which focused on implementing technology to drive specific business outcomes instead of just taking orders.

Somehow I had to convince people to trust me that it was safe and actually advantageous to change to this more proactive model. I needed to be able to *influence* both parties to see things my way. If I failed at either end, we'd have to part ways.

■ ■ ■

The Oxford American Dictionary defines influence as the "capacity to have an effect on the character, development, or behavior of someone or something, or the effect itself."[1]

Leadership, goals, and influence expert Dr. Heidi Grant said the core of influence is trust. More importantly, she said, it's the ability to project trustworthiness. Three simple ways to demonstrate trustworthiness are:

1 Look like you are listening. This means making eye contact and demonstrating that the person speaking has your full attention. It also means not scrolling through your phone or checking your email while on a Zoom call.

2 Express empathy. It doesn't have to be mushy or overly personal. Just acknowledge what the other person is experiencing. It can be as simple as saying, "That sounds really hard."

3 Be candid. Tell people the whole truth even when you know they won't like it. This one is hard because our job often involves telling people things they don't want to hear.[2]

> **↗ The *influence superpower* is the ability to affect or change someone or something in an important way by fostering trust through listening, empathy, and candor.**

■ ■ ■

As part of my new goal and proactive vision, I got a coach. He was amazed that anything worked because it was all so messed up. He complimented me for being present and open, and told me the way I showed up was probably mitigating some of the consequences of my bigger problems. I looked like I was listening because I was listening. The flip side is that I really notice when others aren't truly listening. (Maybe you do too.)

When people perceive you to be listening, they are more likely to pay attention to your recommendations and suggestions because they feel like they are being heard. I would go so far as to say making people feel heard is a Caxy competitive advantage, as well as our deep empathy for not only the roles of our clients but also the people living them.

Starting with some small talk—about sports, kids, family, how we grew up, music, etc.—creates a connection that allows people to relax. Being in a relaxed state makes them more receptive to hearing your hard questions. When you stop talking and start listening, they can hear themselves think and feel safer in divulging what the real problem is.

We worked on one project where we interviewed with a CIO in a rare RFP situation. I was trying to promote our lead developer as their point person, but he just wasn't connecting. The meeting started to go badly, and during a break the guy who had brought me in took me aside and said, "Mike, this is your show. We liked you in the beginning. Would you take this home?"

Thinking back, the developer was doing a fine job listening, and, at least on the surface, empathy didn't appear to be a big factor. The problem was the developer wasn't able to be as candid as he needed to be about the limitations and problems involved in what this organization was asking us to do. Being candid is scary, but hedging or stonewalling is the quickest way to erode trust and tank your influence. I took back the reins, and we got the project.

The business's or customer's needs have to be up front. That means you have to make sure you're solving a problem worth solving. The hardest situation we face is when a client has a preconceived technology solution in mind that isn't based on a desired outcome, but rather on a project to deliver something or a box to check off a list. Worse, a lot of times the client has already decided what the project should cost based on their gut feeling for how long a project of that size might take. It's rare that the business starts with a problem worth fixing, so it's your job as the tech leader to help connect the dots to lead to an outcome.

Another area where candor is essential is when you are dealing with senior leadership. You need to become a resource who can help them think through the size and impact of what they are asking for. You need to help the C-suiter prioritize and make sure what they are asking for is actually going to advance their goals. If they are someone who spits out requests to the technology group sprinkler style, you need to be the one to ask where on the priority list the ask falls. Otherwise, your group will treat it as the first priority, whether it is or not. You need to be able to shift out of technology mode and into business mode on a dime and focus leadership on how the solution they're asking for (or you're presenting) ties into the business.

Most leaders appreciate getting candid feedback they can use. They know who the yes-people are. Being the sole contrarian (if it's justified and you can offer another solution) is not necessarily a bad thing.

In this next story, TR Srikanth, executive in residence for the Technology Association of Oregon and former CIO of Banfield Pet Hospital, describes how he increased his influence exponentially by building and expressing empathy for both customers and staff members working in the business.

The Power of Empathy

TR Srikanth

When it comes to succeeding as a technology executive, what has helped me most is the focus on empathy and real customer needs—meaning really understanding the customer's perspective.

When I was CIO for Banfield Pet Hospital, I had the luxury of having both internal and external customers. However, it really doesn't matter who your customer is. The key is really understanding what they are asking for and what they really need—yes, sometimes there can be a difference between the two. Your empathy can guide you to what they need rather than what they are asking for. You can tell great stories and surface amazing possibilities, but empathy is the underpinning of everything.

A first step toward empathy is to be there whenever possible. Being at *gemba*, as some lean practitioners would call it, allows you and your team to understand the ask, how it is going to solve the problem, and how much is good enough. At Banfield, I was probably one of the first senior IT leaders to wear scrubs and work in the hospitals. A lot of my predecessors had visited, but I was one of the first to be there like an intern, to try and understand the goings-on. I worked at the front desk to understand what a customer service representative (CSR) did with the applications my team had developed. I also worked in the treatment area, holding a pet as they were clipping its nails or drawing blood. I even mopped the floor in the evening, which was part of the daily routine.

Back in our luxurious offices, we still complained about small stuff, but I said to my staff, "Listen. You need to go to the hospital and work in the back. There are like 10 dogs there, and they've peed and pooped all over the place, and the staff is cleaning it up, and they are doing all of it with a smile. The CSRs and staff don't complain. They are focused on the dogs and cats in need. So, before we complain, let's remember those associates who are not in the best of conditions but still passionately serve our customers."

I sent a few people from my staff to shadow folks in the hospitals, directly listen to feedback, and then look at possibilities. They came up with ways to automate a lot of the processes. One example was the patient exam sheet. Previously, when a client checked in, they were given a blank form and asked to fill in their name, their pet's name, etc., which the CSR would then key into our records. The problem was that most of the information captured was static, such as name or gender. By printing out the data from our records on the check-in form or exam sheet, we saved two to three minutes per visit. That efficiency translates to a lot of time saved across a thousand hospitals with an average of 18 visits per doctor per day. It adds up very quickly! 👤

Influence Is about Values

Long ago, I instituted a policy that a failure on any one of our company values equals a *total* failure. You can't hold onto someone because of an illusion that they are such a great producer, but they aren't honest.

Or that they are such a good teammate, but they regularly fail to meet commitments. If you rate someone on your values on a scale of 1 to 5, anything below a 4 is a reason to part ways. A 5 means you exemplify the value. A 4 means you usually do. Do you really want someone on your team who sometimes is a 3?

Speaking of company values, here are Caxy's. Feel free to steal any and all of them for your department. They have served us well. (If you adopt or adapt any of them, I'd love to know.)

1 Be a great foxhole companion. Create a culture where being there when you're needed matters.

2 Own outcomes. Care about the outcome you committed to, and be the person who comes through to make it happen.

3 Seize opportunities to grow. If you're not growing, you're falling behind.

4 Get hyped about the unknown. Be excited about ambiguity and coming up with ways to make something concrete.

5 Speak and listen fearlessly. Be able to say something and give feedback when needed. And be open to receive it.

In terms of culture, being candid (No. 5) is a big deal at Caxy. Speak and listen fearlessly and do it right away, as soon as it's professionally acceptable.

Holding people accountable isn't always easy. When someone runs afoul of a value, you have to be willing to have that hard, honest conversation. Otherwise, it's just words trapped on a page. For example, some years ago there was someone on the path to senior leadership who was leading a big project, but they didn't do enough to hand it off before going on vacation. Worse, they were unreachable. The team that inherited it discovered the deliverable—which they thought was going out that afternoon—wasn't going to be ready until the next month. It was a huge miss.

When the employee got back, I knew we would have to have a serious conversation and one of two things would happen: 1) they would quit on the spot, or 2) they would get it together and be in top leadership by the next year.

I'm happy to report that this person was very moved by the realization of how badly they had let their team down. They turned it around and were promoted into leadership a year later. The toughest obstacle was repairing trust with their team. That's a bridge that takes a while to rebuild.

That said, in my experience, it's incredibly rare for people to recover. As a leader, one of my challenges is to act on my knowledge that it's time for someone to go. It's natural as a person to want to help your team members along. I can only think of a few cases where a performance improvement plan (PIP) really worked. The more you lower your tolerance for team members not living the company's values, the infinitely higher the caliber of the team becomes.

Taking these steps made our team better right away. This person might have seemed untouchable. But values are for everyone, and if you let it slide, the problem will grow. The actions we took were a signal that we expected everyone to live by those values, that it wasn't just a poster on the wall.

■ ■ ■

One area where we as technology professionals have to be candid is explaining the true cost of what the business or client is asking for.

Most business leaders don't have a way to think about the total cost of a software product. They tend to conceive of it in concepts they are comfortable with (design, development, testing, etc.) and tend to omit others that are less on their radar (research, support, technical debt, etc.).

In the next story, Eric Lannert, CTO of Chicago-based cloud-solution company Cloudbakers, does a great job of explaining what technical debt is, what its implications are, and how being candid about what it's going to take allows business leaders to make the most informed decisions possible (even when they don't like what you have to say).

The Courage to Be Candid
Eric Lannert

Often our software development clients will come to us and say, "We absolutely have to have this capability." If we just say "OK" and go off and do it, it doesn't work for a lot of reasons.

This is particularly true in the world of application development. We have to be able to push back. Part of our job is to explain what the true cost of what they are asking for is going to be. We have to help them realize there's more to it than the cost of building it today. They need to account for the future costs—for example, technology updates, maintaining customizations, or future enhancements.

It's called *technical debt*, and when you build something, it's part of the deal. To account for it, we advise clients to factor in 15 percent of the original development costs for the first few years, which over time will grow to 25 or 30 percent.

The problem is clients often are thinking only about what they need today. So our job is to help them see the whole of what they're signing up for, meaning that every customization they require is going to come with a long tail of expense.

When you're in the thick of weekly release cycles, it's pretty easy to try to move at the speed that the client wants. It's way harder to slow things down, be more thoughtful, and explain the true costs and underlying capabilities there.

It also can be challenging when you have different personality types and different levels of responsibility on the client team. It works best when the financial person is there, because they'll be able to comprehend it and say, "Whoa, wait a minute. That's X dollars per year forever. That's bad. Is it really worth that?"

It's also good to have a businessperson there who can say, "Well, yes, it is, because this part of the business is embedded in the process. We hit this every single day. So if we do this capability, it's going to reduce friction on the spinning engines of our business. Therefore, it's a fundamental thing, and we predict it will deliver value that is consistently above and beyond the technical debt it will create." Or, conversely, "This is an expensive thing that we only do twice a year."

The business starts to have that dialogue back and forth about cost and value, thinking about value in terms of frequency and reducing high-frequency friction versus something that's just annoying—something that, in a perfect world, should be automated, but the reality is you shouldn't spend the money to automate it because it's not done often enough to warrant the technical debt.

Some of the toughest conversations we have are with clients moving from a highly customized system to a packaged system that has some customizations on it—for example, something like Zoho, which is a cloud-based office suite with a ton of productivity tools. The problem is they are used to a world where they could come up with an idea or a need and all they had to do was pay a developer to implement it. They had total flexibility, unlimited customization, and the ability to access any piece of data, at any point in time, in any process—that is, a custom application.

When you move to a packaged system, you just don't have that, which is actually a good thing. That's part of the reason it works long-term, because you're not adding all this technical debt for things that are very easy to do. But you had full flexibility and customization, and now you don't. It's a big adjustment. If we've done our jobs, however, we'll have asked all the why questions and the client will have thoroughly thought through the long-term implications of each path, and that's all we really can hope for. 👤

■ ■ ■

Increasing Influence

Some people seem to come by the influence superpower naturally. For example, if you take the DiSC personality assessment and your score for the "I" or "influence" personality style is high, it means you are someone who tends to place an emphasis on shaping the environment by influencing or persuading others.[3] According to the DiSC website, "I styles are motivated by social recognition, group activities, and relationships. They prioritize taking action, collaboration, and expressing enthusiasm and are often described as warm, trusting, optimistic, magnetic, enthusiastic, and convincing."

If that doesn't describe you, don't despair. You can still be influential; you'll just have to focus on projecting trustworthiness and then lean on a few other superpowers to get the job done.

You can do that because the influence superpower actually works best when teamed up with other superpowers. (Think Power Rangers, Transformers, Voltron, or the Powerpuff Girls.) For maximum effectiveness, it should be combined with the superpowers of storytelling, listening, and learning. Don't worry; we'll explore these three superpowers in more detail in Chapters 4, 5, and 6. For now, here are some basic guidelines:

1 **Storytelling superpower: Explain what's in it for them.** To influence effectively, explain to the person how your proposal benefits them or their goal so they can believe in what you are trying to accomplish. Watch your body language and tone of voice. If you're slouching or short with people, no one will be focused on what you have to say.

2 **Listening superpower: Listen before persuading.** Listening to the other person, connecting with what's important to them, and putting it in the context of what you are trying to achieve can have a synergistic effect. The other person can contribute to and even improve the vision. And once that seed is planted in their heart, they will have the drive and ability to spread the word and influence others.

3 **Learning superpower: Establish yourself as an expert.** Speaking and writing are powerful ways to establish industry credibility. You don't have to make the big stage; writing consistently for the company blog, appearing as a podcast guest (or starting your own), and conducting informative webinars all create a trail of expertise that will pay dividends later. What does this have to do with learning? Well, there's no faster way to expose holes in your knowledge than to try teaching it to someone else.

Using Influence for Good

The influence superpower is like a laser tool. You want to be mindful of how and where you aim it. First, you want to be truthful. Whatever you're advocating should be genuinely in the business's best interest. If it's not, you will eventually be found out and that will destroy trust.

Dr. Heidi Grant said that being more influential is actually about *projecting* trustworthiness. It's not necessarily *being* trustworthy! This dark side of influence is called *coercion*. Coercion shows up in a bunch of different ways in the workplace, but if you see people following directives even though they know it won't achieve the stated objectives, that's a big clue. Use that influence superpower for good!

Invest in Building Relationships

Another way to increase your influence (especially if you're more of a just-the-facts type) is to invest time in building connections and relationships with your counterparts across the business—before you need to ask them for anything. Figure out who the influencers and decision-makers are around the company, and go on a listening tour to find out what their pain points are.

Then, when the time comes, it will be easier to get people to listen because you've paid it forward. If you do this, you might find you only have to tell your idea to a few key people to get buy-in. If you are convincing enough, they'll help you get the word out and that will help it stick. Think famous social-media influencers who became darlings of advertisers due to their huge following. Caveat: Advertisers are learning that influencers who endorse anything and everything ultimately lose that trust and eventually their endorsements become meaningless and thus ineffective. When it comes to influence, being perceived as trustworthy is *everything*.

Influence and Stakeholders

The ability to influence is critical to your ability to execute your vision. There are three main groups you'll need to influence: leadership, IT staff, and users (internal or external customers).

The influence superpower is what will allow you to sell a technology initiative to leadership and get funding for it. Depending on the size of the initiative, there likely will be more than one team, composed of people who may or may not report directly to you. The influence superpower also refers to your immediate team, meaning the people you can hire and fire.

Influence Immunity

There will be times when no matter how closely you listen, how much empathy you express, and how candid you are, you won't be able to move the needle. How you react to that depends on which group you're dealing with.

Fire the Unhappy People

When it comes to your staff, if you can't get them on board, you have no choice other than to replace them with people who can be influenced. Some people are just chronically unhappy and obstructive. A post by Jay Goltz in the old "You're the Boss" blog of the *New York Times* described my situation perfectly. Jay runs a number of retail stores in Chicago that cater to the home-improvement and decoration customer. They are lovely to be in and have a great atmosphere.

In the post, Goltz was recounting a conversation he had at a party where people were talking about how nice it was to be in those stores and how amazing it was that the teams got along and were so pleasant to work with. They asked what he did to make that real. Was it training? A checklist of how to be nice to customers? Some kind of magic potion?

Goltz couldn't answer, and it haunted him for a while. And then it hit him. It was simple. He fired the unhappy people.

You can't make people happy, and you can't really even make them productive. You really can't *make* people do anything. It has to come from inside. You need to provide your team with the tools and support systems they need to be successful, but if it's not working out, everyone knows it. In fact, a big part of your job as a leader is to make sure the really good people stay and help the people who aren't cutting it find somewhere else to work—even if you have to make that decision for them. Firing someone is a stressful event, but you'll be amazed at how much better everyone will feel once it has been done.

What does this have to do with influence? Everything. To earn the trust of your staff, you need to move the unhappy people out of their orbit. Your best performers will be happier (and more productive) when you surround them with people who want and deserve to be there.

I know it might sound like I've always operated this way, but nothing could be further from the truth. In fact, I tolerated a combination of unhappy, toxic poor performers and prima donnas for years before I'd finally had enough and moved the unhappy people out—all the way out.

Actions Speak Louder Than Words

In my other life, I'm a musician who has been in bands since I was a teenager (I play guitar and sing), and I can tell you there is no place where trust is more crucial to the outcome than making music.

In my 20s, I was in a band where everyone had great chops both musically and lyrically. We could trust one another both individually and during band rehearsals to do what was needed to be able to perform well once we were on stage. We also loved one another's company. The result was we were a great band that people loved to come out and see. Life and other circumstances broke that group up, but if any of those guys ever called for help I'd give it without hesitation. Why? Because year after year those people always did what they said they were going to do, and more.

I've also been in bands (briefly) that had a lot of problems. There is perhaps no more painful experience than spending time rehearsing and playing with people whose main agenda is to be the center of attention rather than to be part of a group. (By the way, those were usually the same people who, at the end of the night, disappeared when it was time to break down the stage.)

In this next story, John Scholvin, former CTO of a Chicago-based proprietary stock-trading firm and a field consultant at a Boston-based enterprise data software vendor (and also a terrific guitar player), talks about some of the other elements you can employ when building trust, including body language and tone.

 What You Say Matters

John Scholvin

From the very first day you step into a leadership role, people are watching you. The casual things you say and the way you carry yourself really matter because they are remembered. They are filed away, for good and for bad. It's not that you have to be overly cautious and never let your guard down. But the things you just kind of say out of the side of your mouth at a meeting or even your posture at a presentation—all of that stuff goes into the file of everybody's memory at a deeper level than you think. Your body language matters. Natural language matters. Tone matters. I figured this out pretty quickly. But I cost myself some capital in the process.

What I've come to figure out is that the people side of it, the relationship side of it, matters way more than almost everything else. If you're a jerk, you're not getting anything done. And if you're getting run over, you're probably not getting anything done either. But if you're a human and look people in the eye, and if you're telling the truth when you can (because they understand when you can't tell everything), it makes everyone's life easier and you're able to be way more effective. 🙎

■ ■ ■

In the end, clients and business leaders will not only listen to what you have to say, but also be looking to make sure your actions align with your words. That and the other things we've discussed in this chapter will determine their level of trust and thus how influential—and effective—you will be.

■ ■ ■

Summary: Influence

■ The influence superpower is the ability to affect or change someone or something in an important way by fostering trust through listening, empathy, and candor.

■ The influence superpower is amplified by all the other superpowers, especially storytelling, listening, and learning.

■ The opposite of influence is coercion. Don't do that. Use your powers for good.

■ To foster trust, which leads to influence, proactively build relationships across your company.

■ Some people are immune to influence; if they are part of your staff, you may have to make some changes.

■ Actions speak louder than words.

■ Watch what you say because people notice everything. Something you say without thinking may be taken the wrong way and you'll lose their trust.

Storytelling

Iwas once on a call with a prospective client in the publishing business who said they wanted us to create an online version of their print magazine. The client pictured it as an exact digital replica of the magazine—cover, masthead, columns, card inserts, wraps, same layout, etc.—because that's what they knew. Their goal was to increase subscriptions, and they thought providing readers with a way to consume the magazine online was a way to do that.

I didn't disagree that putting the magazine online would help their cause, but I knew the direct-transfer approach wouldn't deliver on their objectives. We talked a while longer, but they weren't hearing me. Somehow I needed to make them realize that print and online were two different mediums, and that one was not going to transfer exactly to the other. And more than that, there were so many additional things they could do if they got the app right.

Then, I had an idea. I said, "OK, so think about other magazines you read on your phone. Do those other magazines use a magazine format?"

"No."

"Why don't they? Why wouldn't it work?"

Crickets.

I continued. "OK, so when you're trying to go through the news, think about the first two swipes. Where would you put that beautiful pull quote?"

More crickets.

"When you're selling a paper magazine," I said, "you don't know what people are reading or how much time they are spending on each page. Online gives you all of that. Think about the potential for recommendations—because you'll know who is signed in and reading. Instead of people needing to go to a venue for panels, they could experience it immediately online or after the fact."

Putting the magazine online required thinking about what the magazine was at its core and how it could serve its customers in a different way than it did in print. That's a new kind of thinking. Up until then, the picture of what the magazine was in the client's head was what they had in front of them in printed form. Putting it online was simply putting that online. We had to connect on what could be different.

Finally, after a moment more of silence, they said, "Oh, OK. What do you think we should do?"

This is a very oversimplified example of a larger situation that all technology leaders are facing. The situation is that most business leaders aren't thinking about new ways to use technology to solve customer problems. They typically are thinking of ways to transfer an existing model to digital in one-to-one fashion. But technology is a moving target. It's difficult to keep up with what customers expect and experience with other companies, and it's difficult to understand what's possible now versus just a year ago. That's the job of the technology executive.

The first thing we need to do is educate ourselves about the potential. The second thing we need to do is change the stories we are telling because the old ones—such as "application development is like building a house" or "security updates are like servicing your car"—no longer adequately represent the current state. Maybe they never did. Maybe those examples are actually driving leadership or customers to make the *wrong* assumptions. Maybe we played along because they seemed close enough.

Let's take the car-maintenance analogy, for example. Most non-technical people understand that an oil change is a way to prevent bad physical things from happening to their cars (e.g., salt, friction, or heat). But that leads them to the wrong mental image, which is that a purpose of software updates is to maintain a system's *physical* aspects (e.g., hard drives or switches). While it feels like it should be a great analogy, it can cause problems by focusing on the wrong things.

While there is naturally some hardware wear and tear involved, focusing on this aspect is burying the headline. The real story here is that the underlying technical systems and software are constantly evolving, and updates are needed to keep pace with innovation and protect against security threats. The key is to find the core concept. Here, it's *integrity*. The maintenance you want to do maintains the integrity of the system just like an oil change maintains the integrity of the car. It's just that the source of the integrity of a software system is categorically different from the source of the integrity of a car in the physical world.

That said, even automobiles are changing. Cars are becoming more and more like a software system every day. And, as a result, the maintenance will have to change too. The reason you're upgrading your system software with a security patch is so you're not vulnerable to a hack. Drivers of electric cars (e.g., Tesla) face the same threat and don't want a hacker to take control of their car while it is speeding down the highway.

So, when you're looking at it from the client's perspective, security updates are *not* like an oil change. And application development is not like building a house. It's more like creating an entire world in *Minecraft*, a world that extends beyond physics as we know it. A house built in *Minecraft* doesn't need a solid foundation, and it doesn't need to obey the rules of physics.

We need to evolve the stories we're telling and develop new analogies and metaphors with which to tell them so we can help our stakeholders be open to new ideas and new worlds for which they have no reference. This also means that you and your leadership may need help building a bridge to this new paradigm—and that's OK.

One of the obstacles you'll face is communicating very abstract concepts to people who are recognized experts in something else. To avoid alienating people, you'll need to find a way to get your point across without talking down to them. The only way to do that is through well-told stories and the use of metaphors and analogies.

In this next story, Jay Dominick, CIO of Princeton University, outlines the challenges of telling stories to an institution filled with experts. Dominick's most recent achievement was enabling the 275-year-old institution, which is lauded for its in-person culture and face-to-face instruction, to offer its classes online less than two weeks after COVID-19 sent everyone home in March 2020.

Getting What You Ask for with Stories

Jay Dominick

Once you get in a C-level role, you've got to be able to tell stories that are authentic, empathetic, and get your point across. If you can't, you're not going to be successful. This is a storytelling job; the higher up you go, the more Mark Twain-ish the stories have to be.

At Princeton, I'm dealing with the smartest people in the world. They're all experts in various things, whether it's the senior leadership, the university, or the board. At this level, I'm spending a fair bit of time trying to advocate or inform a board of directors.

Being able to tell a story that is generally understandable, gets your point across, and is compelling is key. That means a presentation to the board on IT security can't be about the technology. It can't be about routes or the details of what's going wrong. It has to be an authentic story about how you're handling something that includes anecdotes and a moral. You have to have believable characters and a plot with a resolution. That's what people are going to judge you on—whether or not you've told a good story about something you've asked them to support.

For example, every year I do a presentation about information security for the board. I know it has got to be the story of what we're doing now: This is why we're here. This is what we're doing. Let me give you a little example. This is how we resolve this stuff. This is what I'm thinking. If something happened, this is how I would approach the decision-making around it. I tell the story of how I would actually solve a problem. I can't just flip through PowerPoint slides or say things like, "We are fully patched for CVE-2020-1234." My audience will just tune me out.

People understand many roles at a company. The CFO pulls up a dashboard with the financial metrics; everybody understands that. The facilities people buy buildings; everybody understands that. The office that recruits faculty puts out fabulous résumés and describes the tremendous talent they're getting; everybody understands that. Most people do not understand what IT does. We're perceived as being too complicated, too expensive, and full of problems, so the immediate reaction to whatever comes up is, "What's gone wrong, and what is it going to cost to fix it?"

The first step is to accept that people don't want to talk about your technology. They want to talk about the outcomes of the technology—what is going to be different, and how their life is going to be better. They don't need or even want to know the details of what will actually make that happen.

You've got to be able to tell the story of why it's going to be good for them, what they're going to be able to do differently, or why what they have isn't working and how the technology you're proposing will fix it. 👤

■ ■ ■

One of the reasons you're in a leadership role is because the business recognized that you are able to speak to nontech people about the benefits of technology without getting in the weeds. In fact, your success as a technology leader hinges on your ability to translate what the business needs to what your technology team needs, and vice versa.

> ↗ **The *storytelling superpower* is the ability to craft and tell the stories that will allow leadership to grasp how technology can advance their business objectives, so they'll be more likely to cooperate and release the resources you need to create what is necessary.**

■ ■ ■

Human beings are natural storytellers, but many educational systems train us out of it.

Following are some storytelling nuts and bolts that can help you remember what you already know intuitively and increase the impact of the stories you're telling.

Let's use penetration testing as an example because no CFO ever wants to pay for that. (Penetration testing is an authorized simulated cyberattack on a computer system performed to evaluate the security of the system.) Your first impulse might be to create a presentation that shows how much test coverage the apps have and walks through the performance logs and security threats. The problem is most executives won't be able to relate to any of that. In fact, the more technical you get, the less engaged they will become because you aren't talking about how this technology affects business operations or revenue.

The remedy to this problem is to explain how this (or any) issue connects to customers, to things the executive understands and cares about, especially risks regarding revenue. To do so, you need to understand the difference between a story and rhetoric. This will require you to shed some of the aforementioned high school English training.

The job of *rhetoric* is to inform or teach through the demonstration of expertise. A *story* is designed to convey meaning. Story takes rhetoric and supercharges it. Here's an example of rhetoric: "If we don't conduct penetration testing, a hacker may do it for us, exposing us to a multimillion-dollar data breach or an outage, both of which could cripple operations and cause us to lose customers. We need to spend the money to get in front of that now so we can avoid a huge potential disaster later."

Though this may be accurate, it could be easily dismissed as hyperbole because it doesn't involve emotions. Telling a story that depicts the potential impact on the business (and the person you're speaking to) makes it real.

The Five Elements of Story

According to Shawn Coyne, book-publishing veteran and author of *The Story Grid: What Good Editors Know*, stories are composed of five key elements:

1 Inciting incident: Something happens. (The server gets hacked.)

2 Progressive complication: Something else worse happens. (The hack gets to customer data.)

3 Crisis: A "no good decision" point where you have to make a hard and uncomfortable "best bad decision" to do something about what happened. (Tell customers their data was compromised and spend thousands in restoration.)

4 Climax: The fallout. (Customers are upset, staff works overtime to fix it, and there is an unplanned expenditure.)

5 Resolution: The new normal. (We need to spend the money on security to be safe.)[1]

Here's an example of a story you could tell that shows that five-part structure in action: "It's 2:00 a.m. I get a phone call telling me we've been hacked, and the server hosting ABC application—the source of 30 percent of our daily revenue—is down (inciting incident). Worse, no one can tell me yet what other systems the hackers gained access to (progressive complication). My team says they think it's going to take at least three days to get us back up and running, and so while they are doing that leadership has to decide what (and how much) to tell our customers and partners (crisis). Come morning, we're all scrambling to figure out how much revenue will be lost and how to minimize the business disruption. PR is trying to help us figure out what to put in the email to our partners and customers alerting them that we've had a breach (climax). Penetration testing can help us avoid this scenario. It's a simulated cyberattack done by people whose whole purpose in life is to stay one step ahead of the bad guys. If we don't do this testing ourselves now, a hacker may do it for us, exposing us to a multimillion-dollar data breach or an outage, both of which could cripple operations and cause us to lose customers. If we invest the $30,000 to do this now, we can avoid potential financial disaster later (resolution).

Including these elements where you can ensures there is a story arc that will engage your listener on an emotional level. If you're familiar with the problem-approach-resolution (PAR) structure that most case studies follow, knowledge of the five elements of story will help you get the most out of these three sections. In this model, the problem contains an inciting incident and a progressive complication, the approach contains a crisis and a climax, and the resolution is the new normal that you're advocating for.

The Power of Comparisons

Another way to get your point across is to draw comparisons. There are many ways to do so, but the three most common vehicles are analogy, simile, and metaphor.

■ An *analogy* is basically a comparison between two things that have something specific in common to make a point. The classic quotation from *Forrest Gump*—"Life is like a box of chocolates. You never know what you're gonna get."—is an analogy. A technology example would be, "Running software updates is like giving a country's central intelligence agency constant briefings. If we don't do it regularly, eventually the intelligence will be out-of-date and it will be easy to compromise us."

■ A *simile* compares two different things in order to create a new meaning and is often introduced with *like* or *as*—"Life is *like* a box of chocolates" or "Running software updates is *like* giving a country's central intelligence agency constant briefings."

■ A *metaphor* uses one thing to mean another and makes a comparison between the two—"Life *is* a box of chocolates" or "Software updates *are* constant intelligence briefings for servers."

So, if you needed a quick way to communicate what penetration testing is, you could use a simile. You could say to leadership, "We already do vulnerability testing quarterly, which is *like* giving someone the keys to your house and asking them to point out all the ways they see that someone could get in. Penetration testing takes it to the next level. It's *like* hiring a professional burglar to actually break into your house in every way possible and then take whatever they can carry. It's the only way we'll ever really know where all the holes are. This also needs to be done once a year because systems are always changing and hackers are always getting better."[2]

A metaphor, on the other hand, might sound something like this: "Penetration testing *is* inviting a benevolent burglar into your environment to steal whatever he can get his hands on and then tell you how he did it."

■ ■ ■

In this next story, Gabriella Vacca, CTO of Sky Italia, a media and communication company, talks about the power of comparisons, not only in communicating to others, but also in gaining a deeper understanding of increasingly complex concepts, something we all are faced with in today's environment.

Connecting the Dots

Gabriella Vacca

When I was in high school, my way of learning was to go deep into a concept and absorb information about the context. It was a very humanities-based approach that I applied to any subject. I didn't just read a poem or story; I also researched the life of the author at that time because I needed to understand what those words meant at that specific time. And so, as you can imagine, study for me was slow compared to other people. For a while I thought, "Oh my goodness, I am never going to make it."

But going deep like that allowed me to connect the dots, to find the common threads among that poem, the author, the history, and so on. And I have applied that approach to learning all of my life. When I studied algorithms in mathematics, for example, I thought about the concept of two parallel lines—how stressful it must be to be a parallel line, to travel together, be close friends and talk to each other, but never meet. On the other hand, a circle is a happy shape. If you're a circle, you go around and around from wherever you are. You see the same thing again and again. It's boring, but it's very nice.

And so, as you can see, everything is a comparison to me. I am always thinking of everything in terms of what else it's like. When I moved to the United States and started to lead people, I understood that the way to reach them was not by telling them what to do, but by earning their trust and access to their hearts and minds. Being less articulate in English than some of my colleagues when I first started, I used comparisons or analogies all the time.

Once, when we had to launch a new product in wireless, the team said, "Oh, we cannot do it." I said, "Listen, we are like a group of people in a boat in the middle of the ocean. There is no helicopter coming our way. And there is time pressure because we have people in the boat who are starving or sick. So if we don't make it in three days, we're going to have a problem."

Other comparisons I often use are an emergency room where doctors have a shared responsibility (teamwork), clear roles (accountability), and focus on the patient (customer orientation); the jungle, where explorers have to work together and fight against a hostile environment that they do not know; or a helicopter view to indicate that you can see things from the sky, but you can't see what is happening within the buildings, so you need to trust your people to make things work in the best possible way.

■ ■ ■

If you're very lucky, your story can actually inform your approach, as Peter Anderson, CTO of gaming and hospitality enterprise Wind Creek Hospitality, describes in this next story.

 The Strangler Fig

Peter Anderson

I was brought in to work on the casino's technology stack because several parts were failing the business's needs. The website and the apps had all kinds of concurrency-support issues, and the on-prem enterprise data warehouse (EDW) system was not working correctly. The EDW would often fail to collect data, and when it did collect data, it was inaccurate.

We spent the first several months looking at the existing technology stack and putting a lot of measurement in place to try to pinpoint the problems and improve each of the individual areas. We got some decent results and some improvements.

But there came a point when we realized that to get things working on the existing technology stack we would essentially need to reimplement all the components of the entire system. And even if we did that, we were unsure if the problems would go away.

The only way to reliably fix things was to start over using modern technologies and approaches, and then, throughout the creation of the new system, pay close attention to performance, concurrency support, and other business needs.

A challenge we faced is that we had an in-flight program that was running the company's online gaming and social casino. We couldn't just shut it all down and say, "OK, we'll be back in three years with a new system." And that's where the strangler-fig approach to replace the old system came into play.

A strangler fig is a species of tropical figs named for its pattern of growth upon host trees. Strangler figs and other strangler species are common in tropical forests throughout the world. They seed in the upper branches of a tree and gradually work their way down until they root in the soil. Over many years, they grow into fantastic and beautiful shapes, meanwhile strangling and killing the tree that was their host. (The strangler fig idea originates from a 2004 blog post written by software developer Martin Fowler, who said, "This metaphor struck me as a way of describing a way of doing a rewrite of an important system."[3])

Using this concept, we identified the key areas of the old system we wanted to revamp with a new approach. As we implemented the new approach, we carefully tested along the way to make sure it would meet the business's needs. We laid out a road map of things that we had to do over time, and we focused on the most important and critical things first. When we went live six months later, only about 25 percent of the system had been rewritten. However, the most pressing problems related to concurrency had been solved. We were still using a good portion of the legacy system. We continued the strategy of sequentially replacing specific items over time. We can now say the entire legacy system has been replaced with the new system, which is built on modern technologies, with very minimal disruption to the business. ▲

■   ■   ■

Another aspect of storytelling is simply realizing that not everyone knows what you know and that you need to communicate. In this next story, George Hoover, former CTO (retired) of what is now known as NEP Group, describes how he and his cohorts helped investors learn the business they had just purchased. You'll notice that this one leans a bit on the vision superpower, in that they had to help the investors learn the business, as well as on the influence superpower, in that the team had earn the trust of the investors by being candid about why the business did things a certain way.

Communicating with Investors
George Hoover

When I joined NEP Group, it was a small company—25 employees and three owners. NEP provides production studios and supports premier content producers of live sports, entertainment, music, and corporate events. The company now has close to 4,500 employees and operates in nearly 30 countries around the world.

The first transition was to go from a little company—where the owners knew not only every employee, but also their skills and abilities—

to the original owners often being less and less involved and having to explain who we were and what we did to a whole new universe of management who may or may not have really understood the business. They may have understood the financial components of it and the rate of return and whether it was a good deal, but anybody who buys a business always wants to figure out how to make it work better.

In the early days, everybody who was already there knew how everything worked, so we didn't need to explain ourselves to anyone. Then new ownership came in and said, "Hey, wait a minute. What's going on here?"

I'll give you an example. In the beginning, NEP provided television-production facilities for broadcasts originating outside of studios and then migrated to other things. But during the private equity due diligence and post-acquisition meetings, the new owners were very interested in understanding costs, pricing, and how the models were built by the sales team.

They were also interested in understanding asset utilization, so they looked at individual high-dollar-value assets we had and how they were used. One of the things that came up were our high-end broadcast cameras, which cost about $200,000 each. I think at the time we owned about 500 of them—a big capital investment.

So the private-equity folks started looking at prior sales orders and use of the cameras. At one of our early board meetings, they were really excited because they thought we could sell about 200 of our cameras. Based on the sales volume, they assumed we didn't need them all. They said, "We looked at Tuesday and Wednesday and most of the cameras aren't working then. Maybe a hundred cameras work on Friday, then another hundred on Saturday, maybe 150 on Sunday, and then it drops off again. So it really looks like you only need 150 or so cameras."

Well, one of the things we realized we hadn't explained well is that cameras that are at a college football game in Atlanta on Saturday can't be at another college football game in Seattle the next day. Nor can one camera be at a Sunday night football game in Miami and then at a Monday night football game in New England. You had to consider travel and set-up time, which we just knew to account for when scheduling. Naturally, they were disappointed, but it made us realize that we weren't doing a good job of conveying why things were done a certain way (and why their ideas wouldn't work).

Another issue was that, in our work-order system, some cameras appeared to be rented for only two days, which implied that they were not making any money the rest of the week. However, our scheduling system showed that when the cameras were in transit from Seattle to Miami, for example, the client was paying rent for those cameras during the move from point A to point B. This caused us to go back and look at all the things we took for granted because we knew the business and it didn't scare us—and then fix all those things.

Here's another example of something we took for granted. In our business, we move a lot of equipment around the country. Most of it moves in trucks. We made a decision early on that we were going to own the trailers because that's where the equipment was installed, but lease the tractors. Investors would say, "It doesn't seem like a sound investment to lease tractors. Why don't you just buy them?"

The answer we gave them was this: If we own them, we have to maintain them. We have to take care of them. And the first time we don't make it to a Sunday night football game, we lose that contract. We lose our credibility. So we need a very strong partner who can make sure we can get to where we're going. If we have a contract that's worth $300,000 for this weekend, it's well worth it to spend a little insurance money to make sure we get there on time, for the same reason that we wouldn't risk trying to ship those cameras out of Miami on Friday and hope they get to Seattle on Sunday for the game. Because if they don't, our name is mud.

You have to change your thinking about investors to, "Hey, this person has a lot of money invested. How are we making them feel that it's a good investment?" Then you have to minimize the risks and explain the unknown or hidden risks that they may not be aware of. This not only lends to your credibility of decision-making, but also demonstrates that you really understand the business and its resources.

They also need to feel comfortable talking to you at a technical level. You want them to feel comfortable saying, "Explain to me how this works," in a way where they know they're getting a straight answer and have confidence you're not trying to scam your way into spending $50 million on a pipe dream. Every investment group has run into that situation. So, naturally, based on their experience, they're initially going to be a little leery and looking for red flags. You need to earn their trust. ▲

■   ■   ■

Sometimes earning trust is a matter of taking a risk to make a connection by sharing an experience that goes beyond your business role and demonstrates who you really are. In this next story, Dr. Candace Hayden, senior vice president of information technology, North America, at Hutchinson, shares how opening up to her peers with a very personal story brought the management team closer.

 # Stories That Connect People
Dr. Candace Hayden

Our CEO has executive staff management-alignment meetings on occasion, and at this particular one there was an exercise where we were supposed to tell a story—something about yourself. The story had to be not only something personal, but also something that no one else in the organization knew about you.

Most of the management team already had a relationship with someone else on the team when they started with the company. On the other hand, when I started, I knew absolutely nobody. To help people get to know me better quickly, I decided to tell a *very* personal story, which I won't share here. The point is that when I was done, the entire team said, "Wow, we had no idea that you had that particular experience."

As a female in the organization who is an executive and also an African American, sometimes I can be on the outside. My story gave my peers an opportunity to actually get to know Candace the person, beyond Candace the executive, who they've worked with for years. We'd always been cohesive from the standpoint of working together, but we didn't really have a relationship. Once they knew a little bit more about where I was coming from, that's when the relationship really started. 👤

■　■　■

And sometimes it's about the story you tell yourself.

One day in 1939, George Bernard Dantzig, a doctoral candidate at the University of California, Berkeley, arrived late for a graduate-level statistics class and found two problems written on the board. Not knowing they were examples of unproven statistical theorems, he assumed they were part of a homework assignment, jotted them down, and solved them.

Six weeks later, Dantzig's statistics professor notified him that he had prepared one of his two "homework" proofs for publication, and Dantzig was given coauthor credit on a paper several years later when another mathematician independently worked out the same solution to the second problem.[4]

In this example, Dantzig was operating from a "how can I?" mindset, so the story he told himself was that the equations were solvable. What story are you telling yourself about the problems you're encountering?

■　■　■

Summary: Storytelling

- The *storytelling superpower* is the ability to craft and tell the stories that will allow leadership to grasp how technology can advance their business objectives, so they'll be more likely to cooperate and release the resources you need to create what is necessary.

- Stories consist of five elements: something happens (inciting incident); something else worse happens as a result (progressive complication); a "no good decision" point where you have to make a hard and uncomfortable "best bad decision" to do something about what happened (crisis); the fallout from that decision (climax); and the new normal, or what you should do to keep it from happening again (resolution).

- An analogy is a comparison between two things that have something specific in common to make a point. "Life is like a box of chocolates. You never know what you're gonna get."

- A simile compares two different things in order to create a new meaning and is often introduced with *like* or *as*. "Life is *like* a box of chocolates."

- A metaphor uses one thing to mean another and makes a comparison between the two. "Life *is* a box of chocolates."

Listening

"That's closer, but not quite it," said the director of a Chicago-based nonprofit who had invited us to pitch what they had described as a new website. I could tell she was getting frustrated, and I was a bit frustrated by that point too. After about half an hour of discussion, it became clear to me that what she wanted was a lot more than just a website for teachers and students.

It wasn't her fault. I'd walked into the meeting with a preconceived notion of what this project was going to be based on my extensive experience with nonprofits. Then, I had unwittingly accepted her description of a solution rather than starting with the problem. Worse, it had just taken me 30 minutes to realize I should have left those assumptions at the door. I needed to ask questions that would allow me to figure out what problem she was trying to solve with this website.

"Be curious, not judgmental" is a motivational quotation often attributed to Walt Whitman. That is to say, instead of passing judgment and thinking you understand a situation completely, be open and curious. Ask questions. Find out what you don't know. It was time to turn my curiosity up to 11.

"Let's take a different tack," I said. "Imagine this website is done and your students and teachers sit down to use it. What do you want them to be able to do that they can't do now?"

Her eyes brightened. "If I'm a student, I could go on the site and sign up for an account and connect with a teacher. Then the teacher could issue different challenges, and I could respond. Kind of like Facebook," she said.

I sat back in my chair. What she was describing—except for the ability to log in, create a profile, and post some things other people could see—was nothing like Facebook. But Facebook was the perfect touchstone to reference for us to begin to understand one another better. She couldn't put her finger on it, but it felt like that clue was the right one to give me. And she was right.

Wait, I thought. Could she be describing a *platform*?

It was worth a shot.

"OK, so if I'm a student, I can log in and register for a challenge. I can get my assignments online and submit them to an instructor to get feedback and then see my grade at the end. If I'm an instructor, I can log in and see who is registered for my class, issue challenges and assignments, award badges for different milestones, and send students a link to a survey so they can tell me how I'm doing. Is that closer?"

One of my favorite books is *Never Split the Difference* by Chris Voss. Voss is a former FBI hostage negotiator and a recognized expert in high-stakes negotiations. He said that the goal with any conversation is always to get a "That's right," which is evidence that the person feels heard.

The director said, "Yes, that's it. You got it."

> The *listening superpower* is about using all of your senses to take in and parse what is going on around you. It's noticing and responding to what you think others are seeing, thinking, doing, and feeling—not just what they're saying.

■ ■ ■

Between listening to (and looking at) people on Zoom calls for hours on end, listening to podcasts in our leisure time, and listening to our family members about how their day went, you'd think we'd be pretty good at listening. But research shows that we actually only remember between 25 and 50 percent of what we hear.[1] That means if you talk to your boss for 10 minutes, chances are they will only remember about three and a half minutes of that conversation. Conversely, if someone is giving you directions or presenting something, you're probably only getting a piece of it too. Is it the most important piece? How would you know?

A way to get better is to practice *active listening*. Active listening is a technique where you make a conscious effort to hear not only the words that another person is saying, but also the complete message being communicated. Here are six key techniques you can use to develop your active-listening skills:

1 Give the person speaking your undivided attention. Remember the "Look like you're listening" piece of activating the influence superpower? Active listening takes that a step further to *actually* listening, not just looking like you are. Resist the temptation to begin formulating a rebuttal while they're speaking. Observe the person's body language. Are they relaxed? Tense? What is the message they're sending and how does it correlate with what they are saying?

2 Do something on occasion that shows that you're still listening. This could be as simple as nodding your head, smiling, or simply saying, "yes" or "uh huh." Another powerful statement is, "You said X. Talk more about that."

3 Listen for one keyword in their story and repeat it. Them: "The big issue was that we weren't getting throughput." You: "Throughput?" Then listen as they take that anchoring idea and go even deeper.

4 Reflect on what was said and rephrase what you heard. Ask clarifying questions.

5 Avoid interrupting the speaker, even if it seems like they are taking forever to get to the point. Some people are very quick verbally. Others might need time to figure out how to say what they want to say. Allow the speaker to finish their thought before you respond.

6 Be open, candid, and honest in your response, but always do it respectfully.[2]

What about the other side of this equation, which is to get people to listen to *you*? According to psychiatrist, executive coach, and consultant Mark Goulston, author of *Just Listen: Discover the Secret to Getting Through to Absolutely Anyone*, a way to get better is to shift your focus from concern about what they are listening *to* to what they are listening *for*.

For example, if you are going to appear on a podcast or a webinar, and you're focused on what people are listening *to*, you'll focus on the content you're delivering prompted by the bullet points on your PowerPoint slides. When you focus on what people are listening *for*, it becomes about what they need to get out of their interaction with you. The podcast host, for example, is listening for you to say something that makes their listeners go, "Whoa! Wow. Hmm . . . Yes!" Then they'll tell 10 other people about the podcast and insist they need to listen. The host is also listening to you, sure, but what they are really interested in is the value you're providing to their audience.

The other thing that Goulston recommends is to focus on being compelling before you try to convince people of anything. He suggests trying to avoid answering questions for as long as possible, opting instead to ask clarifying questions and then concluding, if possible, with an affirmation of how much they've shared with you. Then request a day to process the information you've collected and do some research so you can come back with the best answers.

If you start to convince too soon, Goulston said, the other person will nod and smile but they won't feel heard. They won't feel felt.

He attributes this result to the function of mirror neurons. A *mirror neuron* is a neuron that fires both when it acts and when the animal observes the same action performed by another animal. Thus, the neuron "mirrors" the behavior of the other, as though the observer were itself acting. Such neurons have been directly observed in human and primate species and birds.

Communications break down when there is a mirror neuron gap. Wide gaps trigger stress, which leads to a rush of cortisol, which is an express train to a brain response of fight, flight, or freeze. This outpouring of cortisol activates the amygdala—the emotional part of the brain—which shuts off access to upper thinking. Things like sarcasm or having to have the last word—all of these things widen the gap.

What you want to do is close that gap, which triggers oxytocin. Oxytocin is a bonding hormone that counteracts cortisol. When people feel felt, the mirror neuron gap closes, and you're able to have a constructive conversation with someone you were chippy with before.

Caveat: There are a ton of listening courses and frameworks out there now and many of them are good, but—especially if you're using this approach with senior management—you better act like you *actually* care what they are saying. Otherwise, they will recognize what you're doing and it might backfire on you.

Another powerful level of listening, said Goulston, is noticing. One of Goulston's mentors was vaunted organizational consultant Warren Bennis, who said that the best leaders were *first-class noticers*—a term borrowed from Saul Bellow's novella, *The Actual*. That means they pay close attention to what is happening around them. Noticing is powerful, said Goulston, because it connects you to whatever you're noticing.[3]

■ ■ ■

In this next story, Rob Isherwood, CEO of South Carolina–based AMBAC International and former CTO for Atlanta marketing agency 22Squared, shares how noticing and then repurposing technology habits that agency employees already had helped improve communications across the company.

The Great Game of Communications

Rob Isherwood

While I was an IT director at 22Squared, we rolled out chat as a tool inside the company. At that point, we had two primary offices, one in Florida, the other in Georgia, and a few satellite offices scattered across the United States—about 1,000 users in all.

Today everyone knows what a powerful team-connecting tool chat can be, but at that time it was a new concept and people didn't gravitate toward it easily or naturally. In fact, very few people used it at all. Around this same time, multiplayer network-based games started to come out and everybody was playing *Call of Duty*. I went in and convinced the executive team to enable people to play *Call of Duty* across the local area network. Why?

In any network, one node is irrelevant and two nodes are completely useless. But a thousand nodes? Now you've got my attention. But how do you get from one to two to a thousand? That's a big chasm. You need something that can pull the team across it. Games do that.

We opened up the LAN to gaming, and people began to play tournaments across departments and between offices. It sounds like a really inappropriate use of corporate resources. But what I did, by using game technology, was build cross-office teams where players went from playing games to using chat to communicate with one another about work-related issues. It created new relationships across departments and built bridges between the two main offices and the satellites so the company could start to behave like one organic being.

As a technologist, I knew connection was powerful, and that the value of a network increased with the square of the number of connections. Now, as a business leader, I can tell you the more interconnected a company is, the more valuable it is.

Did I know this strategy would work? No. I had a rough choreography in mind for what I wanted to have happen. I really didn't know how the elements were going to play together or what piece of it would move me in the right direction—or the wrong one. I couldn't know. But I did know the direction was what I call "roughly right and fast."

I didn't know for sure if deploying games as a way to create an interoffice network would work, but I did know that a) people really enjoy playing games, b) games connect people, and c) I could do it very quickly. In other words, I knew I was roughly right and could put the idea into practice fast. That "roughly right and fast" approach has served me well through many other experiments I've conducted successfully over my career as both a CTO and CEO.

As CEO of AMBAC, I implemented *The Great Game of Business* because I like to play games.[4] The technologists I like to work around are all playing games. Everything is a game to them. If you look at the history of computers, the time from the first transistor to the first game was not very long. Computer games were actually there before spreadsheets!

In fact, the people I've worked around who are really great at applying technology to business problems, and who are great technologists from a business leader's point of view (i.e., really great at driving technology that transforms businesses), share one thing in common: they are like enthusiastic kids.

They're very positive, they're generous to an unbelievable fault, and they're very trusting. They can see the possibilities. "If I connect you to you to you, something amazing will happen. What? I don't know. But it will be amazing!" If I were hiring a technologist, I'd hire that attitude and then teach the skills. It's an attitude that comes from a sense of "the best is yet to be." 👤

■　■　■

In this case, Isherwood wanted to improve communications across the company. But no one walked into his office and said, "Hey, why don't we leverage the chat function that we're not supposed to have but is already in place around here?"

That wasn't possible because people were playing these games discreetly. What Isherwood did was notice this pattern and reorient it to the agency's advantage. He listened to what was going on around him. Of course, to get management to agree to this rather unorthodox solution, Isherwood had to lean on the vision and influence superpowers, but with their help, he was able to achieve his goal.

In this next story, TR Srikanth, executive in residence at the Technology Association of Oregon, talks about the importance of noticing what's going on around you so you can adjust and take action.

■　■　■

👤 Noticing the Trends

TR Srikanth

A lot of people misunderstand agility for speed. It's not about speed. It's about how you respond when a curveball comes in. The people who are coming out of this COVID situation in a better way are the ones who walked through some scenarios, were paying attention to what was happening around them, and quickly took action.

I'll give you an example. A colleague of mine was a CIO managing a global team. In January 2020, he noticed a lot of network equipment, firewalls, and VPN concentrators were being deployed in China.

He was somewhat perplexed by this abnormal behavior pattern. He also noticed that people in his Chinese facility were working from home more and more. Not understanding what was happening or coming, he decided to shore up his network infrastructure in order to provide remote-working capability. And boy, was he right! He took a calculated risk on the purchase, which allowed him to provide a seamless remote-work solution for his associates. Being agile, looking for leading indicators, and acting on calculated risks saved the day for this CIO. ▲

■　■　■

Chances are, you're probably already very plugged into what is happening around you. The challenge is to begin listening to what those patterns and trends are trying to tell you so you can act on those insights to your benefit.

Another listening situation you've probably found yourself in is a one-on-one meeting with an employee who has a problem, where they are waiting for you to tell them what to do. The easy path is to tell people how to do things—or do the thing yourself. In this next story, Dr. Candace Hayden—senior vice president of information technology, North America, at Hutchinson—talks about how she empowers her staff to solve problems by asking questions.

Empowering Staff with Questions
Dr. Candace Hayden

One of the things I like to do instead of showing what I know is ask questions. There's a way to phrase a question that puts the person at ease so they can answer it and you can gain some knowledge based on their answer.

The goal is to get the person to engage with you. Showing what you know is very easy. For example, even though I haven't programmed in years, all of our programmers can come into my office and say, "You know, I'm struggling with this concept. I don't know what to do with it." I have to remember to be in my listening mode and not my get-it-done mode because I'm not the one doing the development. But it's a skill set I have, and it's also something I like to do, so it would be easy for me to give them the elbow and say, "Hey, just let me do this."

Instead, we sit down together, whether it's a storyboard or just a conversation. Rather than giving them the answer, I help them conceptualize where we're trying to take the code so the train of thought develops through them rather than coming from me.

I will step in when necessary, but it depends on the severity of the issue. I watch for that deer-in-the-headlights look. If there's an issue and all I'm getting is stares back, that's my cue to kick in and go "OK, let's just get it done."

■　■　■

Another challenge that many leaders face when they are the highest-ranking person in a meeting is the tendency to interrupt and redirect the conversation, which basically shuts everyone else down. In this next story, Greg Woodard, CEO of Solve, a business-intelligence consultancy, shares how he and his partner overcome this challenge.

Solicit the Opinions of Others before You Speak
Greg Woodard

I recently noticed that when my partner and I attend a meeting and someone starts to talk, we tend to interrupt and redirect them, something like, "No, no, no. This is what we're going to do." The problem with that is all conversation then stops. So now, when I'm holding meetings, I try not to say what I think, but really solicit everyone else's opinion first. As soon as I give my opinion, everyone goes quiet and no one wants to contradict me. It's that old saw— listen more, talk less. You've got two ears, one mouth. They should be used in that ratio. 👤

■   ■   ■

One topic that always comes up when working with clients on software is users—meaning whether to listen to them and, if so, to what extent. Inevitably, someone quotes Steve Jobs, who famously said, "It's not the customer's job to know what they want." And this always bugs me because it's not actually the whole story. By the time Jobs returned to Apple in the 1990s, his view had evolved. He'd been listening to customers for more than 20 years and was deeply attuned to their needs.

In fact, at the 1997 Worldwide Developers Conference, he made this statement: "You've got to start with the customer experience and work backward to the technology . . . I've made this mistake probably more than anybody else in this room . . . As we have tried to come up with a strategy and a vision for Apple, it started with 'What incredible benefits can we give to the customer? Where can we take the customer? . . . I think that's the right path to take."[5]

Maybe you have been listening to customers and users for a long time and are already attuned to their wants and needs, but we've always found it's better to take the time to check with them just to be sure. They might just surprise you.

In this next story, Mark Baldino, cofounder of Fuzzy Math, a Chicago-based user-experience design firm, weighs in on common missteps around interpreting user feedback and explains how to listen to users in a way that will help you deliver a product that allows them to achieve their goals and you to drive desired business outcomes.

👤 Listening to Users

Mark Baldino

The days of business analysts working with only business leaders to gather information and figure out where the market is—and then producing requirement documents in a vacuum that may or may not be what the end users really want or need—are done. When it comes to software development, it's no longer OK to bypass the user. In fact, bypassing the user can be a recipe for failure.

Here's what usually happens. The businesses or tech teams think they have the answers, or worse, they think they are the user. This happens a lot in internal teams that are very technology driven and whose tools have been designed and built by technologists. The technology is typically really, really good. What they don't understand is the difference between what users *say* and what they might really *mean*.

For example, one thing we hear a lot from businesses and technologists is, "Our users or customers are telling us that it doesn't look good." That makes them think the only fixes required are aesthetic ones. What they don't realize is that the way something looks is almost never the core problem. What that statement means nine times out of 10 is that there are usability issues. There are other red-flag keywords that are indicators of deeper problems. "We need to fix the workflow," for example, is a big one.

Another issue is that many developers are comfortable with a lot of data in front of them and with processing that data, so they build tools that work for them because they assume someone like them is going to use the tool. To be clear, there are situations where people are OK with that, and may even insist on it. Health-care systems, particularly hospitals, are one example. Clinicians want a lot of data on the screen, and they don't want to be constantly clicking or scrolling. We've also done some ERP tools for people who work on the factory floor. They have a decent-sized screen because they also want all of that data in front of them.

In most other industries, however, this is not the case. There's plenty of research to show that people are fine with scrolling through pages and they want a little bit more white space. The problem is the mindset of the business and developer, which is often, "I'm capable of anticipating the needs of the user without talking to them." So what happens is they design without a complete picture of what the user is going to need, and the resulting product can't deliver what it needs to deliver.

The predicament gets even worse if the business then wants to grow and scale the tool, perhaps to make it self-service or software as a service, or if it has a high-touch solution that's really technical and wants a broader group of people to be able to use the tool.

Another challenge is that sometimes what needs to happen is the business needs to change how it is doing things to become more efficient. That can be really hard to hear, especially if you've come into the conversation believing that the problems can be solved with a re-skin. That challenge often coincides with times of great change in an organization. Maybe it has acquired another company or has a release it wants to do, which requires a lot of changes to the tool.

Where it gets really difficult is when development or technical expertise has a stranglehold on the entire product organization. In that case, we can focus on small wins. We can keep applying our process and aligning ourselves with the technology leaders, but unless the business can somehow break free so something different can happen, there's not much we can do.

The biggest wins are when we have advocacy within the technology or product team and they understand that a change is needed. They're exasperated, they're being asked to do too much, and they can't keep up, so they are open to trying something different. For example, we were doing a user-experience (UX) design for claims software for a large health-care provider in the United States. We invited some of the development team and some of the executives to monitor how their claims-processing team worked. What we tried to do was conduct interviews and then allow the claims processors to do their work in real time in context. We tried not to interrupt them, and then we asked some questions at the end.

During one specific interview, one of the claims processors mentioned two things right in a row. One was that they had a quota of how many claims they had to process in a day, let's say 50. The other was that if they got two claims incorrect within a six-month period, they lost their job. It also took six months to train on the software. The executive knew about the training period, and that was part of the reason they had brought us in. It was taking too long, and they wanted us to figure out how to fix it.

However, they had never heard that there was a quota. One of the executives stopped the session and said, "Well, first of all, we're going to have to change all of our KPIs for this project because what we're going to do is inevitably going to increase the time it might take for somebody to process a claim. We'll need to adjust those KPIs not only for the business and all of its components, but also for the individuals processing the claims."

Executives also were not aware of the severity of the consequences for improperly processed claims. They knew how it impacted the patient, the provider, and them as the payer if a claim was not processed correctly, but they didn't understand the personal impact of that misstep on the claims processors. This caused a big shift in terms of how this client wanted to approach the project and how they wanted to set their goals and expectations. Because we were allowed to observe the claims processors using the software to do their jobs in real time, we could zero in and fix the real problem. ♟

■ ■ ■

Listening to users will provide you with a lot of data. Just know that data may also contain a lot of noise. For example, users who are also customers may want something from you that you've decided as a business not to do, which is not only OK, but also smart.

On the other hand, they may want things from you that actually make sense but you don't provide or you do provide but they just don't know it. The more data and feedback you get from users and customers, the more you can make smart decisions about what to do next.

The trouble starts when leadership decides it already knows the customer and doesn't need to do any listening. And maybe that's true—today. But over time, what your customers want—and even who your customers are—will shift. So if you aren't listening to what is being said and felt outside of your four walls, you are going to end up selling to a statue that you carved a long time ago.

To stay in touch with users so you can respond appropriately to current needs (and begin to anticipate what they might need in the future), it can be helpful to lean on a UX strategy expert, such as Sandy Marsico, CEO of Chicago-based UX strategy firm Sandstorm Design. In this next story, Marsico talks about the peril of prioritizing your goals over the user's goals when it comes to e-commerce website design.

Whose Goals Come First?

Sandy Marsico

Something that often comes up with clients is what to do with the hero image on their home page. Almost every client wants to fill that space with a rotating banner full of content.

We've done more than 3,400 hours of UX research and usability studies. What we know is that, in the user's mind, the hero image registers as an ad, so they skip it and go to the section below. In fact, the most engagement-rich section of a home page is actually right below that big hero image. So the hero image could be experiential or focused on brand messaging, but it's not the area that actually drives activity because the user knows they are being sold to. The exception to this rule is if you're an e-commerce site because, in that case, you *are* selling to them. The point is users know when you're prioritizing your goals over theirs.

We conducted usability testing on an air-filtration website that showcased the company's four product lines. When users saw the comparison chart of products available, they assumed that, from left to right, the products would go from least expensive to most expensive (or, the opposite, from most to least expensive). Human nature expects an incremental order.

This company ordered its product line three, one, two, then four. Why? Because it wanted the user to buy more of product number three. But selling more of product number three was *their* goal, not the user's goal. The user wanted to compare the four products. They wanted to understand the differences so they could make an informed decision.

Here's what else can happen. Let's say product number three was the third-most expensive option. Because it was listed first, though, users assumed it was the cheapest. You just lost the possibility of selling two alternative products that may have fit their budget. One way to get around this problem is to simply create a callout as a "featured product" or "best seller." There are so many ways to solve it other than tricking the user.

Bear in mind, this wasn't an unethical company or unethical marketers or an IT issue. They weren't out to deceive the user. The business just wanted to sell more of that particular product. The problem is the user gets confused, and then they often don't feel comfortable buying *anything*. All trust goes out the window and any sale you might have made goes with it. ♟

■ ■ ■

As you can see, the listening superpower is a bit of a shapeshifter. It takes many forms and is applied in different ways depending on who—or what—you're dealing with. When you listen:

■ Your team members can tell you who is working out and who is not.

■ Your salespeople can tell you where the friction points are in the acquisition process, and your sales data can tell you which kinds of customers are successful and which are not.

■ Your CEO can tell you whether or not your vision is aligned with theirs.

■ Your CFO can tell you what monetary impact your efforts are having on the business.

■ Your direct reports can tell you how things are going.

■ Your users and customers can tell you what works and what doesn't, and give you a sense of what you need to prepare for in the future.

The point is you can find out much of what you need to know to be successful by getting better at wielding the listening superpower's many facets.

Summary: Listening

■ Be curious, not judgmental.

■ The *listening superpower* is about using all of your senses to take in and parse what is going on around you. It's noticing and responding to what you think others are seeing, thinking, doing, and feeling—not just what they're saying.

■ Practice active-listening techniques—i.e., give the person speaking your undivided attention; do something to let them know you are still listening; ask clarifying questions; avoid interrupting; and be candid but respectful in your responses.

- Instead of focusing on what people are listening *to*, focus on what they are listening *for*.

- Focus on being compelling before you try to convince anyone of anything.

- Pay attention (i.e., listen) to an employee's existing technology patterns to see if they can be repurposed to improve something in the company.

- Keep your eyes and ears to the ground regarding external trends—and trust your instincts.

- To get the best out of your staff, try being the last person to speak in a meeting so you don't shut down their creative thinking.

- Know that there may be a difference between what users *say* and what they might really *mean*. For example, if a user says the interface doesn't look good, there could be usability issues.

- Users know when you are prioritizing your goals over theirs, and it doesn't end well.

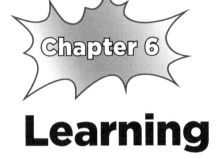

Learning

I was browsing books at Hudson News at the Las Vegas airport after a woefully unsuccessful experience at the 2001 Consumer Electronics Show. We'd spent our last dime on a booth to promote our services creating animated marketing CD-ROMs for companies, and the only person who stopped to talk to us in five days was the comedian Gallagher's brother, who said he thought our business was crazy. (Crazy bad or crazy good? I'll let you decide. I still don't know. I just knew something had to change.)

In the middle of the airport bookstore a book on web development caught my eye. I bought it and read it on the plane ride back to Chicago.

On Monday, we ditched the CD-ROMs and became a web-development company. (True story.) Since then, Caxy has reinvented itself several times in response to where we saw things heading and in alignment with the advice of hockey great Wayne Gretzky's father Walter, who told his son, "Skate to where the puck is going, not where it has been."[1]

The result is that we are always learning as a company, primarily through seeking out projects that force us to solve new problems with new tools. We fearlessly recycle what we do into the next thing, hopefully well before it's everyone else's thing too.

For example, we're knee-deep in machine learning and IoT because we saw it coming and made the learning investment early. Why? Because it's where the business is going.

The great thing about any new technology is that on Day 1 the small guys and individuals are just as good at it as the big guys. It's a new "blue ocean" and everyone has the opportunity to succeed.

That means you have to always be learning about new technology so you are up to speed enough to determine, "OK, has this problem already been solved by an existing app or system I could purchase, or have I found a blue ocean I can sail into?" It's going to look bad if you spend several years and thousands or millions of dollars building something that you could have purchased from a vendor for a fraction of the price.

If you've been in your role for more than 10 years, I urge you to take a step back and look at where you are in terms of "where the puck is going." The consequences of an "if it ain't broke, don't fix it" mind-set could be catastrophic. We fear for the health of the careers (and the companies) of some CIOs we know whose systems are running on legacy software that is 10, 15, or 30 years old because we know there will come a day when they'll be forced to pivot and they won't be able to turn the boat fast enough.

The companies and technology leaders I know of who employ the learning superpower (and others) have had inevitable upward trajectories. They're light. They're nimble. And they're not afraid to change things.

That said, there's one other possible outcome of maintaining the status quo. The company may not go out of business; it may just stay the same, or it may slowly shrink. Think a $50 million company that declines to a $7 million company over a matter of five or six years. It deflates slowly, like a birthday balloon, which slowly descends until it drops to the floor. We've seen it happen.

On the other hand, the upsides of embracing growth can be significant. We just had one client exit for nine figures. That's the model

I want for you, but to get there you must be educated enough to understand what's happening around you and connect whatever technology you choose to a specific business outcome.

> **The *learning superpower* is the ability to effectively respond to an environment of constant and rapid change through the acquisition of new ideas, skills, and mindsets so the company, your team, and you retain the wherewithal to benefit—not only from what is, but also from what's to come.**

■ ■ ■

Technology really is moving faster than ever. We used to talk about Moore's Law, but now it's Ray Kurzweil's Law of Accelerating Returns, which says "We won't experience 100 years of progress in the 21st century—it will be more like 20,000 years of progress (at today's rate)."[2]

Think about the technologies, platforms, partners, languages, and other tools available to you now compared to this time last year. The changes are not only continuous; they are relentless. Moreover, each new tool has the potential to either add value to the business or become a costly distraction. You need to be able to make an informed decision on what new tools or programs will best advance the business outcomes related to your firm's business strategy. To do so, you'll need to make a continuous effort to acquire new knowledge.

Your team should always be learning too. Yes, times are tough and training and development is often the first to go. I get it. The problem is that the evolution of technology waits for no one. That's why everyone on your team needs to be held accountable for constantly expanding their knowledge. With so much knowledge online, and so many vendors eager to establish relationships that could bear fruit later, there's basically no excuse for getting stale. Team members should be actively advancing their knowledge and credentials all the time. Full stop. And even if the business won't pay for formal training, you can still make learning part of your internal culture by rewarding people's efforts, hiring people who are curious by nature, and leading by example.[3]

In this next story, Mark Szkudlarek, vice president, IT strategy and portfolio management, shares how he fosters a learning culture at Novelis Inc.

■ ■ ■

Cultivating a Learning Culture
Mark Szkudlarek

You need to create space for continuous learning in your culture, and that involves creating opportunities for people to engage so you can coach them to think about things differently. Part of that process is including them in meetings where decisions are being made.

In IT, everyone is very busy and will make the case that they don't have time to attend. Also, a lot of IT people tend to be introverts and would rather be left alone to do their work. You still need to invite them. You could say, "There's a reason we invited you to this staff meeting or to this biweekly PMO [project-management office] meeting where we review projects. It's because we really want your opinion and want you to participate."

This can take some reinforcement. After the meeting, you could say, "What are you taking away? What are you learning? How are you adjusting your approach?" A lot of times people don't make the connection until it's pointed out to them.

There are also event-driven learning opportunities, like a new project or a new technology introduction. As part of that project, you can send folks to training or bring in someone who can do a knowledge transfer.

In terms of annual training goals, the company will typically offer some type of leadership skills training. But there should also be process- and technology-related training. For example, IT typically looks to improve its internal delivery processes, training people in agile, ITIL, or ITSM on how to progress work. For a technology example, if you've got an infrastructure person who wants to progress, are you supporting them in acquiring additional knowledge that may lead to certifications, such as a CCNA certification from Cisco or a Microsoft certification? Then, do you encourage and support them to build on that expertise year after year?

You can also decide to build certain expertise internally. For example, we made the decision to train all our employees around security awareness. We developed benchmarks around the role and what classes might make sense. For some people, it was a security essentials boot camp. For one of our stronger technical resources working in IT security, it was a CISSP. By the way, the investment we've made in the security person who is now working on his CISSP is already paying dividends. As we engage with partners and progress with different security initiatives, the deeper skill set he has acquired is making those processes much easier to deliver.

Training is also about helping people find a niche based on their role or where their interests might be, which also helps them do their job better.

Some people make the argument that they don't want to train their people because then they'll leave. My philosophy is, "Hey, if I *don't* train my people, they're going to leave. Worse, if they're not willing to grow, what if they *stay*?"

The other thing to understand is everyone learns differently. I'll give you an example. A couple years ago I coached my 10-year-old's soccer team. We had just moved from Chicago to Dallas. Soccer was one of the things he enjoyed, and we were trying to get him integrated and feeling comfortable about the move. We signed him up and were ready to go. Then suddenly the league said, "I'm sorry, we don't have a coach for this team. And if we don't get a coach, your son's not going to be able to play."

I wanted him to play because I wanted him to adjust to the new city, so I said, "OK, I volunteer"—of course having no idea what I was getting myself into. But here's what I learned. With some kids, you can just throw the ball out there and they start running around and dribbling. With some kids, you can tell them how to do something and they can do it. With some kids, you can say, "Let me demonstrate," and then they pick it up. And then there are some kids who, regardless of how much you share with them or show them, just don't get it, or they're not proficient without a lot of practice.

As I sat there and reflected on teaching a bunch of 10-year-olds with different skill levels how to play soccer, it occurred to me that it was just like work. Some people just know what to do and run out there and do it. Some people need to be told or shown what to do, and then they understand. And then there are some people who, no matter what you do, still don't really get it.

The bottom line is you need to be open and go into it understanding that people learn in different ways. People also are interested in different things, and getting them engaged really comes back to the story you tell them, how you coach them, and how you mentor them.

I like a four-stage training approach where you take an intern or someone new to the role and end up being fairly direct with them, saying, "Hey, I want you to do this, in exactly this way." The next quadrant is, "OK, now you go off and do the work. You come back, and then I'm going to make the decision." The third quadrant is, "OK, you go off and do the work, and then we'll make the decision together." Ultimately, you want people to get to the fourth quadrant, which is, "OK, you go off and do the work, and you make the decision. If you've got any questions, challenges, or issues, let me know, and I'll be happy to help."

All of us, regardless of what tasks or activities we're asked to do, have tasks where we fall into one of the quadrants. In a perfect world, we'd like everybody to be in that last quadrant, where they can just run with it and then come back and ask if they have questions or issues. But not everybody's there, and having that appreciation for where people are in that journey is key. ♟

■　■　■

I see the patterns that Szkudlarek described in my business all the time. But how do you figure out whether the technology person you hire will actually embrace this need to learn all the time? I've found a huge predictor of success is whether the person exhibits *intentionality* around learning. To gauge this trait, when I'm interviewing someone, I look for completed side projects. A completed side project says to me that they were able to conceive of an end goal and then figure out how to build something to get there. (Isn't that what we're all looking for from our tech team members?)

Here's what intentionality around learning looks like in practice. A developer—let's call her Alex—starts thinking through what she wants to build and what it will take to get there. Alex does some searching online and finds a tutorial that looks like it covers at least a portion of what she needs. She works through the tutorial and learns some new things, but that is not her primary agenda. While she is building the tutorial example, she is actively looking for things she can use to build her own project out. As she works, she sees a section she can use for a component she was having trouble with, and then spots another line of code that solves a problem with some database performance that has been happening.

Alex's mindset is grounded in "how can I?" She believes all the information she needs is out there somewhere, and all she needs to do is go immerse herself in it, play around with the ideas, take what she needs, and then integrate it into her own tool kit.

In this next story, one of the many things Yan Pritzker, CEO of Swan Bitcoin and cofounder and former CTO of Reverb.com, talks about is a group of developers who got together after hours to build a digital guitar pedal because they wanted to see what was possible.

The Sound of Software

Yan Pritzker

David Kalt and I founded Reverb.com in 2013, a few years after he purchased Chicago Music Exchange, a brick-and-mortar business that sold musical instruments. To him, the pain point was obvious—people couldn't buy and sell instruments very easily online. There was eBay and Craigslist, but that was basically it.

The reason Reverb.com was so successful was that we understood the purchase of an instrument is a very personal thing. It's very emotional. You're buying something that makes music, not a dishwasher. When people buy an instrument, they want to have a personal experience with the salesperson. They want to feel understood and have trust in the system.

Reverb.com was founded on the idea that we would tell the story of the instrument and let people know we stood behind it. That meant great customer service was always at the forefront of the business. To achieve that level of service, we had to get the right people in place. What we learned was that a lot of people can code, but not a lot of people can code for customers.

One of the things we said in interviews was, "Tell me about a project you were really excited to work on." We then watched for the language they used. Some people would say, "I used this new library and this new coding framework and it was really cool. I got to build all this interesting code." To me, that was a red flag. Are you talking about the end product, or are you talking about the code? I'm a developer and

I love coding, but that's not what should excite you about what you're doing and why you're doing it.

Then there were the people who said things like, "I built this really cool tool for people to use. I had all this interaction with customers and heard all this positive feedback, and here's how I incorporated it." That's where you spot that all-in-one package of product manager and developer. It's showing passion not only for the code, but also for the product you're building.

That is part of the reason why we hired a lot of musicians. If you're a musician, you're building a product for yourself. That's really nice, right? Because you already have that passion. If we found a musician who also was a developer, it was almost always a fit.

We were always looking for tinkerers—people who were solving some software problem or building things in their spare time. It wasn't a make-or-break quality, but we noticed many of the best people were always writing code for something or someone else in their off hours.

One time, a bunch of our developers got together to build an open-source guitar pedal. They found a pedal with a programmable chip, hooked it up to their computer, and started to figure out how to write code for it. None of them had ever done it before (this was around 2016 or 2017; digital effects are more common now). They just said, "Wouldn't it be cool if we could download an effect into this thing?" They would all stay behind at work and make distortions on the computer and download them into the chip. The person leading the project was a musician, but there was another person who was just interested in the idea of an open-source pedal that could change sounds. The cool thing about tinkerers is that if they don't start the project with a personal connection, they ultimately build one through the process. ▲

■　■　■

The ability to learn is particularly essential when it comes to funding new projects. You've got to be able to demonstrate to leadership how what you want to do is going to advance business goals. To do that, you need to not only deeply understand the business—which we've already discussed in Chapter 2—but also learn to speak the language of the person who holds the keys to what you want. In this next story, John Scholvin—former CTO of a Chicago-based proprietary stock-trading firm and a field consultant at a Boston-based enterprise data software vendor—talks about how his decision to learn the language of finance finally allowed him to have a productive conversation with his CFO.

90 Percent toward Them

John Scholvin

As a technology leader for a trading company, my customers were primarily other technologists. I had to provide a plan, market data, and a platform on which they could build the services for the business. For example, if we were building a $5 million hardware plan so a trading desk could do its job, the technologists built it, but I was the guy who would go to the business and say, "OK, I need $5 million."

That meant I had to go ask for money for technical things from decidedly nontechnical people—meaning CFOs and finance people or business side partners—who, upon hearing me say "$5 million," would basically start to shake.

In that case, my job really became about finding their level, finding what language they spoke, and reframing the conversations about technical needs at their level, whatever that might be.

Here's an example. I worked for a trading firm for a long time. The partnership had deferred most of the big gatekeeping decision-making to the CFO, so he was my audience. He was a nice guy and a really good finance guy, but he didn't understand the trading business all that well, which I found a little alarming. Worse, he didn't understand technology at all. It kept coming back to a language problem, and for a very long time whenever I brought him something he said, "Nope, not going to go anywhere."

And it was my boss who said, "If you're going to get anywhere with Bob, you've got to learn how to talk like an accountant." So I did. That's the other thing—you have to legitimately learn their language. You can't just start spewing out word salad, because they'll see it's bullshit. Even though they don't speak your language, they're not dumb.

Eventually I got to the point where, instead of talking about technical requirements, I was able to talk in terms of return on investment and depreciation of hardware assets. I could talk intelligently about financing implications and how we could actually pay for this stuff.

I'd say I had to go 90 percent of the way toward him and he came 10 percent of the way toward me. What I learned was that he was the audience. He was the guy with the money, and I was the guy with the need. If I only went 50 percent of the way there and he was still at 10 percent, there was a 40 percent gulf between us, and I wasn't going to get what I wanted. He's probably an extreme example, but it's a pattern that has come up a couple of times in my career, when I had to not only meet someone at their level, but also move way closer to them and the language they were using than the other way around. 👤

■ ■ ■

You probably noticed that though the point of this example was the need for Scholvin to employ the learning superpower to be able to learn a new language so he could make a connection with the CFO, he also had to employ some of the other superpowers to get his goal over the finish line. First, he had to believe it was possible to connect with this guy, which is about mindset. Then, he had to have some empathy to realize that he would need to be the one to bridge the gap, which is a mashup of the listening and influence superpowers.

The point is Scholvin realized that he was the one who had to uplevel his skills to remain successful.

Key questions: What do you need to learn personally so you don't wake up one day as an obsolete dinosaur or unable to progress in your career? How can you use your personal efforts to learn and stay current and encourage your team to do the same?

In this next story, Sandy Marsico, CEO of UX strategy firm Sandstorm Design, shares her perspective on why technology leaders need to make a personal effort to keep up.

Are You Driving Change?

Sandy Marsico

This might be hard for some people to hear, but 10 minutes into the first client meeting we can tell whether a technology leader is driving change. If they are not familiar with what's new or they talk about building custom solutions to meet requirements that can easily be implemented with proven, off-the-shelf systems, those are big tells. And if that technology leader has been with the company for more than 10 years, they run the risk of being stagnant.

That said, there are organizations where the same person has been in place for 10 years and the company has transformed three times. So leadership needs to look at the past 10 years and make an assessment: How much transformation have we done, or how stagnant have we been? Is there a correlation there? Length of tenure can't be the only data point, because the individual could be helping the organization through a ton of evolution and change.

Do you have a vision for the future, or are you focused on keeping the lights on and making sure everything is running with no hiccups? If things are running smoothly—meaning your server's not down and data is accessible—you might feel like, "OK, everything's good then."

The problem is technology is changing so fast that if you are not going to conferences and events, if you're not taking the time to listen to podcasts or otherwise motivated to grow, it's going to become an issue for the organization in the long term—so lean in now and learn while you still can. 👤

■ ■ ■

My primary goal in this chapter was to spur action, so what I've been talking about thus far is learning that needs to happen *immediately*.

To thrive in the long term, however, will require you to continuously reinvent yourself, advocate for the upskilling and reskilling of your team members, and double down on mastering those things that make you uniquely human, including mindset, vision, influence, storytelling, listening, and learning.

In his book *Hyper-Learning: How to Adapt to the Speed of Change* Edward D. Hess, consultant and professor of business administration at the University of Virginia Darden School of Business, kicks this imperative up several notches. Hess said that keeping pace with technological change requires a new way of being and a new way of working. This new way involves hyper-learning, which Hess defined as "the human capability to learn, unlearn, and relearn continually in order to adapt to the speed of change."

In terms of a new way of being, Hess said that hyper-learning is about becoming your best self—cognitively, behaviorally, and emotionally—and is composed of three steps: achieving inner peace, adopting a hyper-learning mindset, and behaving like a hyper-learner.

Hess said achieving inner peace is a function of four key elements: a quiet ego, a quiet mind, a quiet body, and a positive emotional state. A state of inner peace mitigates the two big inhibitors of learning: ego and fear.

Adopting a hyper-learning mindset involves changing your mindset around who you are and how the world works, and creating a personal story of why you should change.

Finally, behaving like a hyper-learner means identifying seven or eight behaviors that will allow you to assess your current state of competence and what aspects of those behaviors you need to work on. A few examples of behaviors are curiosity, exploration, imagination, open-mindedness, humility, a quiet ego, empathy, courage and candor, and resilience.

A new way of working is about enabling your organization and people to become hyper-learners. According to Hess, the dominant way of working in most organizations today will not enable hyper-learning because it's based on achieving compliance through fear, and fear is a big inhibitor of learning. Hyper-learning requires a work environment that is team-oriented and highly collaborative, not an individual, survival-of-the-fittest, competitive environment.[4]

Hess's book goes into much greater detail about how to achieve all of these things. My objective in getting just a few of its ideas in front of you is to demonstrate a real need for you to embrace and wield the learning superpower—because the future is much closer than you think.

Summary: Learning

- The *learning superpower* is the ability to effectively respond to an environment of constant and rapid change through the acquisition of new ideas, skills, and mindsets so the company, your team, and you retain the wherewithal to benefit—not only from what is, but also from what's to come.

- Create space for continuous learning in your culture by creating opportunities for people to engage so you can coach them to think about things differently.

- Look for the tinkerers—people who were always solving some software problem or building things in their spare time.

- Don't expect leadership (i.e., finance) to learn your language; invest the time to learn their language instead so you can make a connection.

■ If you've been in your role more than 10 years, take a hard look at where you are in terms of the learning curve, so you can upgrade your knowledge and skills before it's too late.

■ Becoming a hyper-learner will require a new way of being and a new way of working.

■ The future is much closer than you think.

Design Thinking

It was that day—the day when the excitement around the desirability of a new project gets dampened by its somber siblings, viability and feasibility. The good news was that, after 20 years of experiencing this predictable phenomenon, we were ready.

Our client, the founder of a software-as-a-service (SaaS) platform, had a vision for what the platform could provide and how it would solve problems for their clients. The first brainstorming meetings were filled with energy, excitement, and the potential of all that could be. In other words, it was the fun part, when you get high on what you think you want without thinking about how you'll deal with reality.

To guide the process to the next level in a constructive way, we shifted our mindset and approach to one of design thinking. We took what we thought we knew and applied the design-thinking principle of empathy. We spent the next few months in an iterative loop of engaging stakeholders and customers to figure out what they really wanted and needed from the new platform the client was envisioning. Then we took that information, thought about some ways we could achieve those goals, and winnowed those ideas further down through a series of thought experiments. Rinse and repeat.

Over the next few months, we used this process to explore what users might want and what tools and content could be built to support them. A number of new technologies and a platform built to solve real problems emerged. The final product was very different from what any of us had originally imagined, but it was so much better because of our process, collaboration, and understanding of the outcome we were going for.

■　■　■

Design and consulting firm IDEO, who was among the first to practice design thinking as a discipline, defines it this way: *design thinking* is a human-centered approach to innovation that draws from the designer's tool kit to integrate the needs of people, the possibilities of technology, and the requirements for business success.[1]

In this chapter, my goal is to show you how design thinking is every bit the superpower that mindset, vision, influence, storytelling, listening, and learning are, and to show you how effective this approach can be when it comes to solving business problems with software.

"To harvest the power of design thinking, individuals, teams, and organizations have to cultivate optimism. People have to believe that it is within their power to create new ideas that will serve unmet needs and that will have a positive impact," said Tim Brown, chair of IDEO. They have to have what you now know is a promotion or "how can we?" *mindset.*[2]

> ↗ The *design-thinking superpower*, according to IDEO, is the ability to bring together what is desirable from a human point of view with what is technologically feasible and economically viable. It creates a solution that will fulfill a *vision.*[3]

Boiled down to its core elements, design thinking is about five things: empathy, problem definition, ideation, prototyping, and testing (i.e., experimentation). It's an iterative process that starts with empathy, i.e., seeing things from the customer's point of view. It involves observing, interviewing, and learning from extreme perspectives to expand your thinking and elicit new ideas, which are about *listening* and *learning.*

It's then about taking those insights and generating bold new ideas through the process of ideation, where quantity rules. Brendan Boyle, founder of IDEO Play Lab said, "Brilliant ideas often seem ridiculous. Ideation time is the time to be playful, embrace wild ideas, and stretch beyond the obvious."

Next up is experimentation. Boyle encourages people to take their ideas—even the wild ones—and build a rough and tangible example of them (a prototype). How quickly can you get something out into the world and start getting feedback? At this point, it's about testing to learn, not to validate.

The final step is to share what you've learned as a story that communicates insights from your research and how people responded to your prototype. The *storytelling* you do around the design-thinking outcome is what will allow you to *influence* others to understand the outcome and respond to your call to action.[4]

In the following story, Rachel Higham, former managing director of IT for a major telecommunications company and current CIO for WPP, shows the full power of design thinking in shifting mindset and solving problems.

Design Thinking in Action
Rachel Higham

I came across design thinking about seven years ago as it was starting to be used outside of its traditional home in product design and enterprise architecture. I thought, "Wow, this is the perfect bundle of practices to not only improve service and product outcomes, but also shift the mindsets of the technology teams building them." Digital transformation is first and foremost about transforming culture, mindset, and behaviors. Design thinking naturally centers on the customer, their experience, and the improvement in their outcomes. If you take design thinking further by also incorporating inclusive design practices, then it really is a special mix.

We adopted design thinking as the central lever of our transformation at the telecommunications company because the IT organization I inherited had become very distanced from the customers it served. Our software engineers were often designing, coding, or testing without a deep understanding of the customers' needs, pain points, or possible moments of despair and delight in their journey.

Design thinking not only drove human and customer centricity, but also did so in a really inclusive way—through ethnographic research, observational research, and co-creation.

We trained 5,500 people across our organization, and purposefully took an experiential approach to that training and coaching. We sent people to weeklong immersion boot camps, where they worked through the methodology in a guided way, with real requirements, challenges, projects, or pain points. By the end of the week, they had a prototype they could take back and show to their customer to get feedback.

During the week, participants were required to deeply research the end customer and validate their hypotheses and their solution options. We started to build that muscle very early on, and then we used that technique in two ways. One was the traditional way of using it to get better outcomes in our new product and service design. The second was actually to design how we worked as an IT organization.

One of the biggest pain points across the organization was the way we provided infrastructure to our software engineers. For example, a software engineer in Bangalore or Brazil would put in an order and it *might* arrive 12 weeks later. We changed the process and now they get it in under two hours, which completely transformed their experience and dramatically improved colleague-engagement scores.

That win came out of one of our first boot camps. We were brain-storming for problem statements, and that pain point surfaced as the strongest theme. The group asked, "Well, how long does it take to get an order?" This led to some research, and we got wildly differing timescales, with an average of 12 weeks. And I thought, "Well, we can do better," so we formed a squad to go solve for it from those who were most passionate about the problem.

The average net promoter score (NPS) of any service that we've sent through this process is +51, which is astounding compared to the NPS of -21 that we got before we started using design thinking. (A net promoter score is a management tool that can be used to gauge the loyalty of a firm's customer relationships. It serves as an alternative to traditional customer-satisfaction research and is typically correlated with revenue growth.) Our highest-scoring services have achieved a score of +88 because we have codesigned the service and the whole journey through it with our customer every step of the way.

The last outcome—which we knew would happen, but not quite to the scale it did—was a cost transformation. The organization had gone through seven years of cost cutting and was fatigued. It needed a transformation that wasn't solely focused on costs—that's one of the reasons we chose design thinking. We knew that if we reimag-ined our services, had our team and customers tell us where we could remove all those clunky manual glue points they found painful in any process, we would get efficiencies. We realized a 38 percent annualized saving on our IT budget over three years even though we primarily focused on improving the experience of our colleagues and customers.

By empowering teams to solve the problems they already knew about but never felt they could address, you can find opportunities to strip out inefficiencies, costs, and barriers to great experience—not by making short-term, cost-saving decisions, but by removing pain points, manual friction and glue, and bad design. ▲

■ ■ ■

Design thinking is becoming more important for software development because it can help development teams better understand both the business problem that needs to be solved and the end users of the proposed technology before any coding occurs. The due diligence of the five-part design-thinking approach allows the development team to learn about the end users and their needs so that when software development does begin it is more focused and efficient.

In the next chapter, we'll circle back to the mindset superpower and reveal yet another one of its most potent facets.

Summary: Design Thinking

■ The *design-thinking superpower* is the ability to bring together what is desirable from a human point of view with what is technologically feasible and economically viable. It creates a solution that will fulfill a *vision*.

■ Design thinking is a process that is grounded in a promotion ("how can we?") mindset.

■ There are five main components of design thinking: empathy, problem definition, ideation, experimentation, prototyping, and testing (i.e., experimentation).

■ Design thinking can drive human and customer centricity in a really inclusive way, which is tremendously useful when developing outcome-focused software solutions.

Mindset (Reprise)

Years ago, I wanted to hand the reins of running the technology group of my company to someone else so I could focus on growth and other activities. I turned to the developer I had on staff, who had a long track record of delivering great work and had the respect of his team and the clients he worked with. When I offered him the job, it sounded great to him. He cared about quality, raising the bar for the team, and the kind of work we were doing.

Thinking that his background was enough to make him successful, I didn't give him much support in terms of training or other skills, and pretty quickly, issues started to pile up. He had gone from developing and being in charge of his own projects to developing and being in charge of *all* the projects. Whenever someone had an issue, he started by giving them some guidance, but then rather than shifting into "how can we?" mode and figuring out how to make the team member better, he got frustrated with their lack of progress and, bit by bit, took over their work. The team started to withdraw and, as I learned later, became fearful of making mistakes to the point of not wanting to do much of anything. Things came to a head when he came into my office, said he couldn't do it anymore, and quit.

Sadly, this was not a new or even a unique mistake on my part. In *The E-Myth Revisited: Why Most Small Businesses Don't Work and*

What to Do About It, a famous book about understanding entrepreneurship, author Michael Gerber tells the tale of a woman who makes the best pies anyone has ever tasted. Her friends and family tell her she should open a pie shop. Who better to start such a business than the best pie baker? But the baker soon realizes that running a pie shop only has a little bit to do with baking pies. It's also about operations, payroll, taxes, marketing, training, hiring, and more. To succeed, the baker has to be humble enough to either undertake things they are not an expert at or hire others who are better at those things to help. I would argue that running any business or department is about humility, which is another important facet of the mindset superpower.

Humility gets a bad rap because in some contexts it implies subservience or even weakness. When it comes to leadership, however, psychological research indicates humility is most closely associated with a cluster of highly positive qualities, including sincerity, modesty, fairness, truthfulness, unpretentiousness, and authenticity. Humility does *not* imply the absence of strength and courage! In fact, it's quite the opposite.[1]

In an article for the *Harvard Business Review*, author and professor of organizational behavior Dan Cable put it this way: "When you're a leader—no matter how long you've been in your role or how hard the journey was to get there—you are merely overhead unless you're bringing out the best in your employees. Unfortunately, many leaders lose sight of this."[2] Cable also said a key to success is to help people feel purposeful, motivated, and energized so they can bring their best selves to work. One of the best ways to do that is to adopt the humble mindset of a servant leader.

The Robert K. Greenleaf Center for Servant Leadership defines the concept as follows: "Servant leadership is a philosophy and set of practices that enriches the lives of individuals, builds better organizations, and ultimately creates a more just and caring world."[3] Pat Falotico, vice president of business development for professional business development and coaching firm Pathbuilders and former CEO of the Greenleaf Center, said, "Servant leadership ultimately starts with an unselfish mindset. If you have selfish motivations, then you are not going to be a good servant leader. It has to be less about you."[4]

Here is one last story, from Linwood "Woody" Ma, CTO of innovative brokerage firm tastyworks. Ma is a great example of someone who not only uses all the superpowers, but also employs the full power of the servant leadership mindset and reaps all the benefits.

👤 Servant Leadership Mindset in Action
Linwood "Woody" Ma

When you're taking charge of a group of people, it's a lot like having kids. You're not the one dancing or playing sports—it's your kids, and your job is to make sure they are the ones in the spotlight. You're just there to help them out. You also have to look at everything you do as an investment in the future, and not just your future—everybody's future.

The challenge is that this approach can be a little hard on the ego. For example, if you delegate something to someone you trust—who understands the task is an investment in the future and gets it done—you may feel like, "OK, am I really important anymore?" Yes, you are. Because your role now is really about teaching the members of the organization to think less about themselves and more about the overall effort, and teaching them that, over time, the investment mindset will pay a dividend. The thing is that the dividend doesn't have to be about you either. Maybe it will be that you made a contribution and built a strong "family" infrastructure in spite of the challenges. Then, whatever ends up happening after that, whether you move on to another role or the company is sold, your team and their roles are secure.

Because after you leave, they'll still need a job. That's the long-term investment there.

There are a lot of pressures and influences that make this type of servant leadership difficult. Navigating it all comes down to one thing, and that is expectations. In fact, the most flexible things in a corporate organization are expectations. I'll give you an example.

Organizations tend to operate in layers. One layer is the doers. They are at the bottom, but technically they are at the top because they're the ones actually doing stuff. Then there are the visionaries. They take ownership in some way, whether or not it's actually their company. They are very high-level people who are making the decisions about how to invest time, money, and resources in the overall organization. And then there's often a middle layer whose sole purpose is to manage things, which typically takes the form of setting and managing expectations between the doers and the visionaries.

Managers are also supposed to be advocating for leadership's vision, but if that vision hasn't been well articulated, or doesn't jibe with their vision—you can end up with different drivers and a variety of expectations floating around the organization. Your role as a leader is to make sure everyone is operating from the same playbook so everyone is tracking to one set of expectations.

Another way to think about expectations is in terms of resources. Let's say I need to buy a new car. I want a Mercedes, but I don't have enough money. In the tech world, the equivalent is that you have all this work you need to do, but you only have a certain number of developer resources. The way a lot of leaders deal with this problem is to drive their people to work harder. But what you really need to do is figure out a way to understand that you inevitably have way more work than you can possibly do, and then just move forward. When that expectation mismatch is removed, people are more honest. And I always say that businesses run better on honesty—they run better on the truth.

That means you've also got to be honest about what is really going on even when it doesn't suit your own best interests. When we started the brokerage firm tastyworks, I was involved because I'd done a brokerage firm before. Like most start-ups, we were all doers. As we neared launch, however, a strong truth began to emerge. It was becoming clear that the technical lead and project manager really deserved to be formally recognized as the CTO, which was normally my role. That led to a personal crisis where I had to say, "Wow, this sucks for me, but you know what? It's actually the right thing to do." That was about the same time I realized I needed to look at the entire situation as an investor. It wasn't about me or whether I was still around. It was about doing my part to make sure the company made the best decisions for its future, and was always seeking opportunities to recognize its team contributions.

Another way this played out was when I brought a software development firm on for a project. (Full disclosure: it was Caxy.) I expected that eventually the business team wouldn't need me to be directly managing the details. What I wanted to do was build up a resource that the business and marketing teams could use directly so I wouldn't have to be involved. I did a little sketch of some technology, handed it off to the developers, and they built it and managed all the pesky details. I was like, "Awesome, this is going to work totally fine." And once again, all of a sudden, nobody cared about me. And that's exactly the way it's supposed to be.

The foundational moment was when I figured out that I needed to be honest no matter what happened to me. If you're not honest with yourself about what's really going on, it's very difficult to make a clear decision. It's really about striving to operate from the truth and making those investments in the company and the people because, in the end, it's not about you. 👤

■ ■ ■

Management legend Ken Blanchard once said, "The reason some people think servant leadership means an abdication of responsibility is that they don't understand the two aspects of servant leadership: vision/direction, which is the *leadership* aspect of servant leadership; and implementation, which is the *servant* aspect of servant leadership."

Both aspects, servant and leadership, are about maximizing the use of the seven superpowers, but the leadership aspect is fueled by the vision superpower. The leadership aspect is about creating that vision, and the servant aspect is about doing what is necessary so your staff can help you bring that vision into reality.

Summary: Mindset (Reprise)

■ The *mindset superpower* is the ability to operate from the mindset that serves you best, including the ability to solve problems by asking "how can we?" rather than focusing on "why we can't."

■ Another aspect of the mindset superpower is humility, which is manifested in an approach called servant leadership.

■ Servant leaders are able to admit that they can benefit from the expertise of others who have less power than them because they know it is the best way to advance their agenda.

Taking Inventory

You now know all the superpowers available to you to achieve more success as a technology leader, but let's face it, that and five bucks will get you a grande latte at Starbucks. The information in this book won't do you any good unless you take action.

You could cherry-pick different activities from the various chapters—and there is nothing wrong with that, especially if you want some quick wins. But let me suggest that this might be a good time to stop and take a 30,000-foot view of where you are overall when it comes to the seven superpowers required for success as a technology leader.

To assist you, I've created a quick diagnostic you can use to gauge where you are in every superpower. Maybe you're strong in storytelling and influence, but weak in vision and learning. Maybe you've got the mindset thing down, but need to work on the storytelling power. Whatever the case, looking at the powers as one unit can be helpful in determining where the most resources are required.

Superpowered Self-Diagnostic

The diagnostic below is designed to assess your current level of overall superpower. Each superpower has three to five questions, and there are five answer choices for each, ranging from "never" to "always." Go through and circle the answer that best fits for each question. Be honest. There's no judgment; in fact, this is a good place for you to invoke your growth mindset. To understand where the best place is to start, you need to know where you stand right now.

Note: You can also take this diagnostic online at https://make mesuperpowered.com/quiz. It will calculate the results for you and provide additional feedback (registration is required).

Mindset

1. My organization operates from a place of "how can we?" rather than "why we can't."

Never   **Rarely**   **Sometimes**   **Often**   **Always**

2. My company culture is "That's how we've always done it."

Never   **Rarely**   **Sometimes**   **Often**   **Always**

3. Leadership insists that technology doesn't matter because the market is unchangeable.

Never   **Rarely**   **Sometimes**   **Often**   **Always**

4. My organization perceives all its people decisions as utilitarian rather than as investments in their future.

Never   **Rarely**   **Sometimes**   **Often**   **Always**

5. My organization leads by command and control rather than by humble servant leadership.

Never   **Rarely**   **Sometimes**   **Often**   **Always**

Vision

6. I have a clear technology vision for my company or department and stay connected to it by revisiting it every week.

Never   **Rarely**   **Sometimes**   **Often**   **Always**

7. I communicate my vision (or the company's vision) to my team at least once a month.

Never   **Rarely**   **Sometimes**   **Often**   **Always**

8. My team understands and resonates with my vision.

Never   **Rarely**   **Sometimes**   **Often**   **Always**

Influence

9. I foster trust by being kind but candid when discussing important issues.

Never   **Rarely**   **Sometimes**   **Often**   **Always**

10. I make an effort to understand what the person I am talking to is saying.

Never   **Rarely**   **Sometimes**   **Often**   **Always**

11. I check in with myself to make sure what I say and what I do are in alignment.

Never   **Rarely**   **Sometimes**   **Often**   **Always**

Storytelling

12. I resist speaking in jargon and referencing only my point of view.

Never   **Rarely**   **Sometimes**   **Often**   **Always**

13. I make an effort to demonstrate the core idea of a complex issue by connecting it to a generalized, understandable concept, such as an analogy or metaphor.

Never   **Rarely**   **Sometimes**   **Often**   **Always**

14. I first identify the business value in what we are trying to accomplish and then create a story around that to get my point across.

Never   **Rarely**   **Sometimes**   **Often**   **Always**

15. I begin my stories with an inciting incident, and there is always a crisis decision point followed by the impact of that decision and the end result.

Never   **Rarely**   **Sometimes**   **Often**   **Always**

16. When I hear a great storyteller, I pay special attention to what makes what they are saying so riveting and try to incorporate those techniques into my arsenal.

Never   **Rarely**   **Sometimes**   **Often**   **Always**

Listening

17. I am present in my interactions with customers and my team.

Never   **Rarely**   **Sometimes**   **Often**   **Always**

18. I make an effort to not bring my preconceived notions to conversations.

Never   **Rarely**   **Sometimes**   **Often**   **Always**

19. I try to understand what the other person is listening for.

Never   **Rarely**   **Sometimes**   **Often**   **Always**

Learning

20. I spend time each month seeking out and developing new skills.

Never   **Rarely**   **Sometimes**   **Often**   **Always**

21. My team has opportunities to learn beyond just doing the work in front of them.

Never   **Rarely**   **Sometimes**   **Often**   **Always**

22. My organization supports the learning growth of team members.

Never   **Rarely**   **Sometimes**   **Often**   **Always**

23. I am willing to do 90 percent of the work to learn another language (e.g., finance) if it means I will be able to get what I need to advance the organization's agenda.

Never   Rarely   Sometimes   Often   Always

Design Thinking

24. I give my team time and resources to thoroughly understand the user and desired business outcome before they start the work.

Never   Rarely   Sometimes   Often   Always

25. Empathy, ideation, and experimentation is part of our software-design process.

Never   Rarely   Sometimes   Often   Always

26. I effectively use the other superpowers to promote the benefits of the design-thinking approach to leadership and customers.

Never   Rarely   Sometimes   Often   Always

Mindset (Reprise)

27. My organization acknowledges the benefits of servant leadership.

Never   Rarely   Sometimes   Often   Always

■ ■ ■

You've probably already figured out where you need to do the most work. However, if you circled "always" for questions 2, 3, 4, and 5 and "never" for any of the rest, those are areas you might want to explore further.

If you would like a more in-depth audit that will produce some specific insights and recommendations, visit makemesuperpowered.com/audit and sign up for a free 30-minute consultation.

Conclusion

I began this project with the intention of creating a book that would provide you with inspiration and actionable advice—things you could put in play immediately to make your job as a technology leader easier and make you more effective on every level. To make sure I understood your challenges, I invited your peers—people who have actually walked many miles in your shoes—to contribute their experiences and wisdom. I hope you found value in it.

If you've made it this far, I want to thank you for investing your precious time and attention in reading this book. I'd love to hear your feedback. Send me an email at mike@makemesuperpowered. com. I'll look forward to hearing your thoughts.

■ ■ ■

Acknowledgments

From the standpoint of a musician, writing this book has been one very long period of writing and rehearsing (almost two years). I want to thank all of the people who helped me conceive and develop this show—you are the reason this book exists, and it's finally ready for prime time.

First, I want to thank the technology executives and business leaders who agreed to be interviewed for this book. (There were more than 40 of them!) Whether or not your content was among those selected for inclusion in the book, please know that you influenced what this book ultimately became. Your input was invaluable and made me a better leader.

I also want to thank Helena Bouchez of Executive Words, my editor and taskmaster, who told me "the book will tell you what it wants to be." Her skills and perseverance are a huge part of what this book is and the fact that it exists at all.

Special props go out to David Bruno, Julie Colbrese, and Tom Schaff—three advisers and coaches whose guidance over the years has influenced my voice and what I find important about being a leader.

To Hannah and Josh Deason-Schroeder and the team at Caxy Interactive, thank you so much for working through these ideas with me over the last several years. We wouldn't be where we are without your insight, intelligence, care, and dedication.

To my parents, Dan and Rosemary, who inspired me to be a better leader with who they are and the work they did, and who were also a sounding board for the book—thank you.

And finally, thank you and love to my family—my wife Angela, and my sons, Rocco and Blaise. You're the reason I get up in the morning. Thanks for listening to me talk about this book over and over again. Thanks especially to Angela for helping me think through the superpowers and stories over the last two years. She has lived the ups and downs in my anecdotes as well.

■ ■ ■

Endnotes

Chapter 1

1. Heidi Grant Halvorson, "Are You Promotion or Prevention-Focused?" *Psychology Today*, March 7, 2013, https://www.psychologytoday.com/us/blog/the-science -success/201303/are-you-promotion-or-prevention-focused.

2. Nassim Nicholas Taleb, *Antifragile: Things That Gain from Disorder* (New York: Random House, 2012,) 20–21.

3. "What Is Design Thinking?" Ideo U, https://www.ideou.com/blogs/inspiration /what-is-design-thinking.

4. Jeanne M. Liedtka, Randy Salzman, and Daisy Azer (authors of *Design Thinking for the Greater Good: Innovation in the Social Sector*), "Develop a Growth Mindset Through Design Thinking," Julie Winkle Giulioni's blog, https://www.juliewinklegiulioni.com/blog/learning-matters/develop-a-growth -mindset-through-design-thinking/.

Chapter 2

1. Christine Rowland, "Telsa, Inc.'s Mission Statement & Vision Statement (An Analysis)," Panmore Institute, August 27, 2018, http://panmore.com/tesla -motors-inc-vision-statement-mission-statement-analysis.

2. Kamil Franek, "Amazon Annual Report: Financial Overview & Analysis 2019," Kamil Franek Business Analytics, last updated September 23, 2020, https://www.kamilfranek.com/amazon-annual-report-financial-overview -and-analysis/.

3. Amazon Mission and Vision Statement Analysis," Amazon, June 19, 2019, https://mission-statement.com/amazon/.

4. Angus Loten, "Average Age of CIOs Nudges Higher," *Wall Street Journal*, January 23, 2020, https://www.wsj.com/articles/average-age-of-cios-nudges -higher-11579791604.

5. Ben Davis, "How Long Does Digital Transformation Take?" Econsultancy, January 22, 2019, https://econsultancy.com/how-long-does-digital-transformation -take-timescale/.

Chapter 3

1. *The New Oxford American Dictionary*, 2nd ed. (Oxford, England: Oxford University Press, 2005), 865.

2. Heidi Grant, "3 Things to Do with Dr. Heidi Grant: Increasing Your Influence," February 2, 2021, https://youtu.be/g1PZXJQlKo8.

3. DiSC® is an acronym that stands for the four main behavioral styles outlined in the DiSC model of personalities: D stands for Dominance, I stands for Influence, S stands for Steadiness, and C stands for Conscientiousness.

Chapter 4

1. Shawn Coyne, *The Story Grid: What Good Editors Know* (New York: Black Irish Entertainment, 2015), 157–159.

2. Emily Boden, "Cybersecurity 101: Vulnerability Assessment vs. Penetration Testing," August 1, 2017, eSentire, https://www.esentire.com/blog/cybersecurity-101-vulnerability-assessment-vs-penetration-testing.

3. Martin Fowler, "Strangler Fig Application," Martin Fowler.com, June 29, 2004, https://martinfowler.com/bliki/StranglerFigApplication.html.

4. David Mikkelson, "The Unsolvable Math Problem," Snopes, December 4, 1996, https://www.snopes.com/fact-check/the-unsolvable-math-problem/.

Chapter 5

1. "Active Listening: Hear What People Are Really Saying," MindTools, https://www.mindtools.com/CommSkll/ActiveListening.htm.

2. Ibid.

3. Mark Goulston, "Learning to Listen," *Unleashed: How to Thrive as an Independent Professional*, Episode 282, starting at 4:14, May 11, 2020, https://www.youtube.com/watch?v=x97uXa1SeIk&ab_channel=WillBachman.

4. *The Great Game of Business* teaches employees to think and act like owners, using open-book management techniques developed by Jack Stack.

5. "Steve Jobs Insult Response," YouTube, 1:53, 1997, https://www.youtube.com/watch?v=FF-tKLISfPE&ab_channel=MikeCane.

Chapter 6

1. Jason Kirby, "CEOs: Stop Debasing Wayne Gretzy's 'I Skate to Where the Puck Is Going' Quote," *Canadian Business*, October 3, 2014, https://www.canadianbusiness .com/blogs-and-comment/stop-using-gretzky-where-the-puck-is-quote/.

2. Peter H. Diamandis, "Why Tech Is Accelerating," Dimandis.com, January 9, 2016, https://www.diamandis.com/blog/why-tech-is-accelerating.

3. Tomas Chamorro-Premuzic and Josh Bersin, "4 Ways to Create a Learning Culture on Your Team," *Harvard Business Review*, July 12, 2018, https://hbr.org/2018/07/4-ways-to-create-a-learning-culture-on-your-team.

4. Edward D. Hess, *Hyper-Learning: How to Adapt to the Speed of Change* (San Francisco: Berrett-Koehler Publishers, 2020), 1, 2, 11, 12, 15, 94, and 166.

Chapter 7

1. "Design Thinking Defined," IDEO Design Thinking, https://designthinking .ideo.com/.

2. Amol R. Kadam, "Design Thinking Is Not a Process, It's a Mindset," *Entrepreneur Middle East*, March 15, 2018, https://www.entrepreneur.com/article/310282.

3. "Design Thinking Defined," IDEO Design Thinking, https://designthinking .ideo.com/.

4. IDEO, five-part email course on design thinking, January 11–15, 2021.

Chapter 8

1. Bill Taylor, "If Humility Is So Important, Why Are Leaders So Arrogant?" *Harvard Business Review*, October 15, 2018, https://hbr.org/2018/10/if-humility -is-so-important-why-are-leaders-so-arrogant.

2. Dan Cable, "How Humble Leadership Really Works," *Harvard Business Review*, April 23, 2018, https://hbr.org/2018/04/how-humble-leadership-really-works.

3. "Start Here: What Is Servant Leadership?" Robert K. Greenleaf Center for Servant Leadership, https://www.greenleaf.org/what-is-servant-leadership/.

4. Mark Tarallo, "The Art of Servant Leadership," SHRM, May 17, 2018, https://www.shrm.org/ResourcesAndTools/hr-topics/organizational-and -employee-development/Pages/The-Art-of-Servant-Leadership.aspx.

About the Author

Michael LaVista is founder and CEO of Caxy Interactive, a Chicago-based software development firm that works with fintech, insurtech, manufacturing, health care, HR tech, higher education, nonprofit, and startup companies to create outcome-based software.

Over the past 20 years, Michael has acted as strategic adviser to dozens of CIOs, CTOs, and CEOs on the development, evolution, and repair of mission- and business-critical software, so he understands those roles as well as the problems and challenges they face.

In addition to running Caxy, Michael is also a musician who plays guitar in a local band. He resides in a northern suburb of Chicago with his wife, Angela, two children, Rocco and Blaise, and their dog, Oliver. For more information, please visit makemesuperpowered.com.

■ ■ ■

Made in the USA
Las Vegas, NV
04 September 2021